# FORMS

# FOLDS

# SIZES

First published in the United States of America by
Rockport Publishers, Inc.
33 Commercial Street
Gloucester, Massachusetts 01930-5089
Telephone: (978) 282-9590
Fax: (978) 283-2742
www.rockpub.com

**Library of Congress Cataloging-in-Publication Data**
Evans, Poppy, [date]
    Forms, folds, and sizes : all the details graphic designers need to know but can never find / Poppy Evans.
        p.    cm.
    Includes bibliographical references.
    ISBN 1-59253-054-0 (vinyl)
    1. Printing—Handbooks, manuals, etc. 2. Graphic design (Typography)—Handbooks, manuals, etc. 3. Packaging—Handbooks, manuals, etc. 4. Shippers' guides. I. Title.
Z244.3.E83 2004
686.2—dc22

                                                                    2003026487
                                                                    CIP

ISBN 1-59253-054-0

10  9  8  7  6  5  4  3  2  1

Interior Design and Layout: Peter King & Company
Cover Design: Stoltze Design

Printed in China

# Forms, Folds, and Sizes

All the Details Graphic Designers Need to Know but Can Never Find

*Poppy Evans*

GLOUCESTER MASSACHUSETTS

ROCKPORT

PUBLISHERS

# ○ Contents

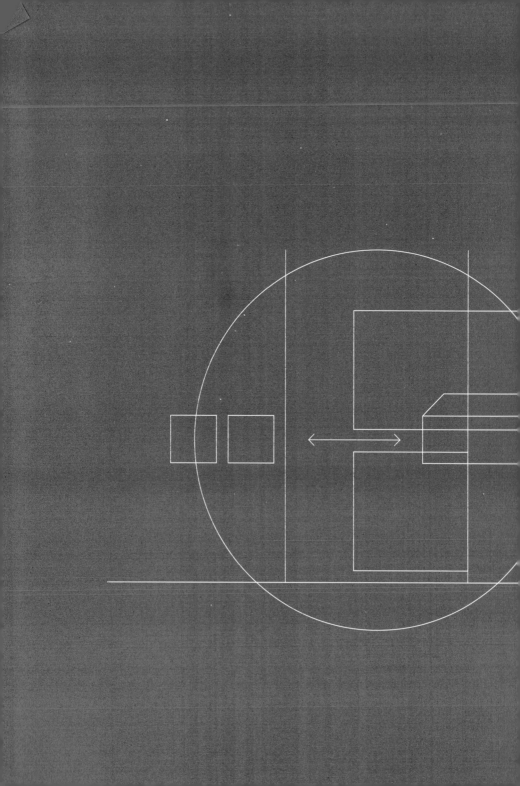

# ○ Introduction

Graphic designers and others responsible for preparing printed materials frequently refer to a variety of diagrams, swatches, templates, conversion tables, and other resources that help them do their job. However, few designers have all the resources they need at their fingertips. Those who work independently, or in small studio environments, often find themselves wasting time searching the Web or seeking out other sources for the information they need. Others in large studio or agency environments may have access to a vast library of resources but find themselves spending just as much time looking through volumes of materials before they find the information they need.

*Forms, Folds, and Sizes* is a compilation of essential information—a reference manual that provides designers with information they need on a daily basis, from consulting a library of type samples to identifying a specific font, to checking the style and dimensions of a specific type of envelope, to understanding when it is appropriate to abbreviate a state or country name in the acceptable format. There's even a bibliography at the end of the book to help, if additional information is needed.

*Forms, Folds, and Sizes* was created to answer the questions that designers ask most often and to deliver this information in a concise, understandable, and easy-to-access way. No frills, no excess—just bottom-line information to help you produce your projects.

## MILLIMETERS, POINTS, AND PICAS TO INCHES

| mm | points | picas | inches |
|---|---|---|---|
| 1.586 | 4.513 | 0.375 | 1/16 |
| 3.175 | 9.034 | 0.75 | 1/8 |
| 4.763 | 13.552 | 1.125 | 3/16 |
| 6.35 | 18.068 | 1.5 | 1/4 |
| 7.938 | 22.586 | 1.875 | 5/16 |
| 9.525 | 27.101 | 2.25 | 3/8 |
| 11.113 | 31.620 | 2.635 | 7/16 |
| 12.7 | 36.135 | 3.011 | 1/2 |
| 14.288 | 40.653 | 3.388 | 9/16 |
| 15.875 | 45.169 | 3.764 | 5/8 |
| 17.463 | 49.687 | 4.140 | 11/16 |
| 19.050 | 54.203 | 4.517 | 3/4 |
| 21.638 | 61.566 | 5.130 | 13/16 |
| 22.225 | 63.236 | 5.270 | 7/8 |
| 23.813 | 67.755 | 5.646 | 15/16 |
| 25.4 | 72.27 | 6.022 | 1 inch |

## INCH DECIMALS TO INCH FRACTIONS

| decimals | fractions | decimals | fractions |
|---|---|---|---|
| 0.063 | 1/16 | 0.531 | 17/32 |
| 0.094 | 3/32 | 0.563 | 9/16 |
| 0.125 | 1/8 | 0.594 | 19/32 |
| 0.156 | 5/32 | 0.625 | 5/8 |
| 0.188 | 3/16 | 0.656 | 21/32 |
| 0.219 | 7/32 | 0.688 | 11/16 |
| 0.250 | 1/4 | 0.719 | 23/32 |
| 0.281 | 9/32 | 0.75 | 3/4 |
| 0.313 | 5/16 | 0.781 | 25/32 |
| 0.344 | 11/32 | 0.813 | 13/16 |
| 0.375 | 3/8 | 0.844 | 27/32 |
| 0.406 | 13/32 | 0.875 | 7/8 |
| 0.438 | 7/16 | 0.906 | 29/32 |
| 0.469 | 15/32 | 0.938 | 15/16 |
| 0.5 | 1/2 | 0.969 | 31/32 |
|  |  | 1.000 | 1 inch |

## CONVERSION FORMULAS

| 1 inch | 2.54 centimeters |
| | 25.4 millimeters |
| | 72.27 points |
| | 6.0225 picas |
| **1 foot** | 30.5 centimeters |
| **1 yard** | 0.9 meter |
| **1 meter** | 1.1 yards |
| **1 centimeter** | 0.03 foot |
| | 0.4 inch |
| **1 millimeter** | 0.0394 inch |
| | 2.8453 points |
| | 0.2371 pica |
| **1 point** | 0.0138 inch |
| | 0.08335 pica |
| | 0.3515 millimeter |
| **1 pica** | 0.166 inch |
| | 4.2175 millimeters |
| | 12 points |

| 1 square (sq.) inch | 6.45 sq. centimeters |
| **1 sq. centimeter** | 0.16 sq. inch |
| **1 sq. foot** | 0.09 sq. meter |
| **1 sq. meter** | 10.8 sq. feet |
| **1 sq. yard** | 0.8 sq. meter |
| **1 sq. meter** | 1.2 sq. yards |
| **1 pound** | 0.45 kilogram |
| **1 kilogram** | 2.2 pounds |
| **1 ounce** | 28.4 grams |
| **1 gram** | 0.04 ounce |

## METRIC TO IMPERIAL EQUIVALENTS

| **25.4 millimeters** | 1 inch |
| **304.8 millimeters** | 1 foot |
| **914.4 millimeters** | 1 yard |

# ○ Chapter 2: Copyright and Trademark Standards

## COPYRIGHT

Copyright is defined as the exclusive legal right to reproduce, publish, and sell a literary, musical, or artistic work. Anything that is produced is a copyrighted piece of work as soon as it is produced if it falls under one of the above categories. In the United States, a work is under the protection of copyright from the moment it is created until seventy years after its author's death. During that period, the owner of a copyrighted work owns the rights to its reproduction, display, distribution, and adaptation to derivative works. (Note that a "work" can be copyrighted, but not an idea. Ideas must be patented.) A copyright infringement occurs when somebody copies a copyright protected work owned by someone else or exercises an exclusive right without authorization.

A copyright notice, strategically placed on literary, musical, or artistic work, serves as a warning to potential plagiarizers. A copyright notice consists of the word "Copyright" or its symbol, ©, the year the work was created or first published, and the full name of the copyright owner.

**Example:** © 2004 John Doe

The copyright notice should be placed where it can be easily seen. Placing a copyright notice on a piece of work isn't absolutely necessary to claim copyright infringement, but it is in the owner's best interest to use this symbol as a warning. Original work can be further protected by registering it with the U.S. Copyright Office:

*Copyright Office*
*Library of Congress*
*101 Independence Ave., S.E.*
*Washington, DC 20559*
*(202) 707-3000 (information)*
*(202) 707-9100 (forms and publications hotline)*
*www.loc.gov/copyright*

Registering an artistic work requires filing an application with the Copyright Office and accompanying it with two visual representations, in printed form, of the work being registered. There is a $30 nonrefundable application fee. Application forms can be obtained from the Copyright Office. The work becomes registered on the date that all the required elements for registration are received by the Copyright Office.

## PUBLIC DOMAIN

Older artistic creations, which are no longer protected by copyright, fall into a category called "public domain," and can be used by anyone without obtaining permission or paying a fee. Uncredited or anonymous works are no longer protected by copyright beyond 95 years after the date of their publication or 120 years after their creation. Works credited to an artist or author are no longer protected beyond 70 years after the creator's death.

## Transferring Rights

Transferring a copyright means granting permission to another to use or publish the work on a temporary basis. Some common types of transfer rights and what is involved are:

*First rights:* The work is leased for one use where it is published for the first time.

*One-time rights:* The work is leased for one use, but there is no guarantee that the buyer is the first to have published the work.

*Exclusive rights:* The leaser retains the right to use or publish the work exclusively in their industry. With an arrangement of this type, an artistic work that appears in a magazine may not appear in another magazine, however it could be used on a greeting card.

*Reprint rights:* The leaser is given the right to use or publish the work after it has appeared elsewhere. Also called serial rights.

*Promotion rights:* The leaser is given the right to use the work for promotional purposes. This type of agreement is often tacked onto another rights contract. For instance, an agreement with a greeting card company to use an illustration on a greeting card would include a promotion rights clause giving the company the right to use the same illustration in its promotion of the card.

## TRADEMARKS AND SERVICE MARKS

A trademark is a word(s), phrase(s), symbol(s), or design(s) that distinguishes the source of a product from one originator from those of another. A service mark is the same as a trademark except that it distinguishes the source of a service. An infringement occurs when somebody uses or mimics an existing trademark or service mark to represent another product or service so that others are misled into believing they are purchasing the original product or service. It is not necessary to register a logo or mark. A user can establish rights with a mark based on its legitimate use. However, owning a federal trademark registration has advantages:

1. Providing legal presumption of the registrant's ownership of the mark and exclusive right to use the mark and the ability to bring legal action concerning misuse of the mark.

2. The right to obtain registration in foreign countries and ability to file the US registration with the US Customs Service to prevent importation of infringing foreign goods.

3. Ability to display notice to the public of claim of ownership through the use of the ® symbol.

Users can use the symbols ™ (trademark) and ᔆᴹ (service mark) to alert the public to their claim of rights to a mark, regardless of whether an application has been filed with the United States Patent and Trademark Office (USPTO). However, the federal registration symbol ® can only be used after the USPTO actually registers a mark and not while an application is pending. The registration symbol can only be used with the mark on, or in connection with, the goods and/or services listed in the federal trademark registration.

Registering a trademark or service mark requires filing an application with the United States Patent and Trademark Office. Contact the USPTO at:

*Commissioner for Trademarks, 2900 Crystal Drive, Arlington, VA 22202-3514*
*(703) 308-9000 (Trademark Assistance Center)*
Registrants can also file online by logging on at:www.uspto.gov/teas/index.html.

# Chapter 3: Proofreading and Copywriting

## PROOFREADERS' SYMBOLS

These marks and notations are widely used and understood by editors, proofreaders, and others involved in writing and producing text. Use them when proofing or editing a manuscript.

| Explanation | Mark | How Used | |
|---|---|---|---|
| Delete or take out | ℐ | *Treasure Island,* by Robert Lewiss Stevenson | ℐ |
| Insert | ∧ | *Treasure Island,* Robert Lewis Stevenson | by ∧ |
| Let it stand | stet | *Treasure Island,* by Robert Lewis Stevenson | stet |
| Close up | ◡ | *Treasure Island,* by Robert Lewis S tevenson | |
| Spell out | SP | *Treasure Island,* by Robt Lewis Stevenson | SP |
| Boldface | bf | *Treasure Island,* by Robert Lewis Stevenson | bf |
| Italics | ital | Treasure Island, by Robert Lewis Stevenson | ital |
| Roman | rom | Treasure Island, by Robert Lewis Stevenson | rom |
| Correct alignment | ⹀ | Treasure Island, by Robert Lewis Stevenson | align |
| Transpose these items | ∼ | Island Treasure, by Robert Lewis Stevenson | tr |
| Wrong font | wf | *Treasure Island,* by Robert Lewis Stevenson | wf |
| Lowercase | / lc | TREASURE Island, by Robert Lewis Stevenson | lc |
| Uppercase | ≡ uc | treasure Island, by Robert Lewis Stevenson | uc |
| Space | # | *Treasure Island,* by Robert LewisStevenson | # |
| Period | ⊙ | | |
| Ellipsis or leader dots | ⋯ | | |
| Begin new paragraph | ¶ | | |
| Em dash | m̅ | | |
| En dash | n̅ | | |
| Move right | ⌉ | | |
| Move left | ⌊ | | |

## FOOTNOTES

Notes and footnotes always end with periods, even if they do not form complete sentences. Source lines do not end in periods. Use the following sequence when listing more than one footnote per page:

*   First footnote
†   Second footnote
**  Third footnote
‡   Fourth footnote

## ABBREVIATION GUIDE

When to abbreviate a word or name and how to abbreviate it will vary, depending on how it is used. Consult the following categories for usage advice on any given term or name and its abbreviation.

### Time Designations

When designating an hour of the day, use figures for clock time followed by a.m. and p.m. Midnight, noon, 12:00 midnight, or 12:00 noon are preferred to 12:00 p.m. or 12:00 a.m. Use AD preceding the year, with no comma (AD 2004); BC following the year, with no comma (115 BC). Use abbreviations for seconds, minutes, hours, weeks, and months in tables and charts only. Spell out in all other situations.

| Meaning | Abbreviation |
| --- | --- |
| after the birth of Christ | AD or A.D. |
| before the birth of Christ | BC or B.C. |
| before noon | a.m. |
| after noon | p.m. |
| century | cent. |
| year | yr. |
| months | mos. |
| month | mo. |
| week | wk. |
| hour | hr. |
| minute | min. |
| seconds | sec. |

## Months of the Year

Use abbreviations in charts, maps, and tables or when they appear with a date and year (Jan. 12, 1935). Spell out in all other applications (January, 1935).

| Month | Abbreviation |
| --- | --- |
| January | Jan. |
| February | Feb. |
| March | Mar. |
| April | Apr. |
| May | May |
| June | June |
| July | July |
| August | Aug. |
| September | Sept. |
| October | Oct. |
| November | Nov. |
| December | Dec. |

## Days of the Week

Use abbreviations in charts and tables only.

| Day | Abbreviation |
| --- | --- |
| Monday | Mon. |
| Tuesday | Tues. |
| Wednesday | Wed. |
| Thursday | Thur. |
| Friday | Fri. |
| Saturday | Sat. |
| Sunday | Sun. |

## United States State Abbreviations

When the name of a US state appears as part of a complete mailing address, use the postal service abbreviation.

| State | Postal Service Abbreviation | State | Postal Service Abbreviation |
|---|---|---|---|
| Alabama | AL | Montana | MT |
| Alaska | AK | Nebraska | NE |
| Arizona | AZ | Nevada | NV |
| Arkansas | AR | New Hampshire | NH |
| California | CA | New Jersey | NJ |
| Colorado | CO | New Mexico | NM |
| Connecticut | CT | New York | NY |
| Delaware | DE | North Carolina | NC |
| District of Columbia | DC | North Dakota | ND |
| Florida | FL | Ohio | OH |
| Georgia | GA | Oklahoma | OK |
| Hawaii | HI | Oregon | OR |
| Idaho | ID | Pennsylvania | PA |
| Illinois | IL | Rhode Island | RI |
| Indiana | IN | South Carolina | SC |
| Iowa | IA | South Dakota | SD |
| Kansas | KS | Tennessee | TN |
| Kentucky | KY | Texas | TX |
| Louisiana | LA | Utah | UT |
| Maine | ME | Vermont | VT |
| Maryland | MD | Virginia | VA |
| Massachusetts | MA | Washington | WA |
| Michigan | MI | West Virginia | WV |
| Minnesota | MN | Wisconsin | WI |
| Mississippi | MS | Wyoming | WY |
| Missouri | MO | | |

## United States Territories

| Territory | Postal Service Abbreviation |
|---|---|
| American Samoa | AS |
| Federated States of Micronesia | FM |
| Guam | GU |
| Marshall Islands | MH |
| Palau | PW |
| Puerto Rico | PR |
| Virgin Islands | VI |

## Nations and World Regions

Use the following abbreviations for maps, tables, charts, and address labels. For other applications, spell out the full name of a country or region.

| Nation or World Region | Abbreviation | Nation or World Region | Abbreviation |
|---|---|---|---|
| Afghanistan | Afgh. | El Salvador | El Salv. |
| Albania | Alb. | Estonia | Est. |
| Algeria | Alg. | Ethiopia | Eth. |
| Armenia . | Arm. | Fiji | Fiji |
| Angola | Ang. | Finland | Fin. |
| Argentina | Arg. | France | France |
| Aruba | Aru | Georgia | Geor. |
| Australia | Austral. | Germany | Germ. |
| Austria | Aust. | Ghana | Ghana |
| Bahamas | Bah. | Great Britain | Britain, G.B. |
| Bangladesh | Bngl. | Greece | Gr. |
| Barbados | Barb. | Guatemala | Guat. |
| Belgium | Belg. | Guinea | Guinea |
| Bermuda | Berm. | Haiti | Haiti |
| Bolivia | Bol. | Honduras | Hond. |
| Botswana | Bots. | Hong Kong | H.K. |
| Brazil | Braz. | Hungary | Hungary |
| Bulgaria | Bulg. | Iceland | Ice. |
| Byelorussia | Bye. | India | India |
| Cambodia | Camb. | Indonesia | Indon. |
| Canada | Can. | Iran | Iran |
| Cayman Islands | Cay. Is. | Iraq | Iraq |
| Central African Republic | C.A.R. | Ireland | Ire. |
| Chad | Chad | Israel | Isr. |
| Chile | Chile | Italy | It. |
| Colombia | Col. | Jamaica | Jam. |
| Congo | Congo | Japan | Jap. |
| Cuba | Cuba | Jordan | Jor. |
| Cyprus | Cyprus | Kashmir | Kash. |
| Czechoslovakia | Czech. | Kenya | Ken. |
| Denmark | Cen. | Kuwait | Kuw. |
| Dominica | Dmica. | Laos | Laos |
| Dominican Republic | Dom. Rep. | Latvia | Lat. |
| Ecuador | Ecua | Lebanon | Leb. |
| Egypt | Egypt | Liberia | Liberia |

| Nation or World Region | Abbreviation | Nation or World Region | Abbreviation |
|---|---|---|---|
| Libya | Lib. | Singapore | Sing. |
| Lithuania | Lith. | Somalia | Som. |
| Luxembourg | Lux. | South Africa | S. Af. |
| Macao | Mac. | South Korea | S. Kor. |
| Madagascar | Madag. | Soviet Union | U.S.S.R |
| Malaysia | Malay., Mal. | Spain | Sp. |
| Malta | Malta | Sudan | Sud. |
| Mauritania | Mauritania | Swaziland | Swaz. |
| Mexico | Mex. | Sweden | Sw. |
| Monaco | Mon. | Switzerland | Switz. |
| Mongolia | Mong. | Syria | Syr. |
| Morocco | Mor. | Taiwan | Taiwan |
| Mozambique | Moz. | Tahzania | Tanz., Tan. |
| Nepal | Nepal | Thailand | Thai. |
| Netherlands | Neth | Trinidad and Tobago | Trin. & Tob. |
| New Zealand | N.Z. | Tunisia | Tun. |
| Nicaragua | Nicar. | Turkey | Turk. |
| Niger | Niger | Uganda | Uga., Ug. |
| Nigeria | Nigeria | Ukraine | Ukr. |
| North Korea | N. Kor. | United Arab Emirates | U.A.E. |
| Norway | Nor. | United States | U.S. |
| Pakistan | Pak. | Uruguay | Uru. |
| Palestine | Pal. | Uzbekistan | Uzb. |
| Panama | Pan. | Venezuela | Venez. |
| Paraguay | Para. | Vietnam | Viet. |
| People's Republic of China | China | Virgin Island | V.I. |
| Peru | Peru | Wales | Wales |
| Philippines | Phil. | Yemen | Yemen |
| Poland | Pol. | Yugoslavia | Yug. |
| Portugal | Port. | Zaire | Zaire |
| Puerto Rico | P.R. | Zambia | Zam. |
| Romania | Rom. | Zimbabwe | Zim. |
| Russia | Russ. | | |
| Saudi Arabia | Saudi Ar. | | |
| Scotland | Scot. | | |

Check the following
guidelines for when to
use numerals or spell
out numbers and dates:

- In general, spell out cardinal
and ordinal numbers below
10 (four days). Use figures
for numbers 10 and up (15
people) unless they begin
a sentence (fifteen people
entered the house).

- Weights, measures, figure
numbers, times, and dates
should always be stated
numerically.

- Numbers that would
normally be spelled out
might get confusing in
sequence. Switch to
numerals when stating
more than one numerical
description in sequence
(he filled 12 eight-oz.
glasses).

- Add an s to numerals
and dates to pluralize them
(1950s, '70s, B-52s).

## Weights and Measures

### UNITED STATES

| | |
|---|---|
| mile | mi. |
| yard(s) | yd. |
| foot | ft. |
| inch | in. |
| ton(s) | t. |
| pounds | lb. |
| ounces | oz. |
| pint | pt. |
| quart | qt. |
| gallon | gal. |
| horsepower | hp. |
| miles per gallon | mpg |
| miles per hour | mph |

### INTERNATIONAL

| | |
|---|---|
| kilometer | km |
| meter | m |
| centimeter | cm |
| millimeter | mm |
| metric ton | t |
| kilogram | kg |
| gram | g |
| liter | L |
| milliliter | mL |
| British thermal unit | Btu |
| calorie | cal. |
| hectare | ha |
| hertz | Hz |

**Common Prefixes**

| Prefix | Symbol | Factor |
|--------|--------|--------|
| mega- | M | 1,000,000 |
| kilo- | k | 1,000 |
| centi- | c | 1/100 |
| milli- | m | 1/1,000 |

## HYPHENATION GUIDE

There are differences in length between the hyphen (-), the en dash (–) and the em dash (—). Each has its proper place in written language.

*Hyphen:* Use in words that are broken over two lines (pro-ject), fractions (a two-thirds majority), multiple modifiers (part-time employee) or as a national combination (African-American).

*en dash:* Use in place of "through" in a numerical sequence (January 23–25, 2001; pages 53–66) or in other designations of time (May–June).

*em dash:* Use as punctuation in place of a semicolon or a colon (The computer industry was in full bloom—many technological methods were well established).

## IMAGE FILE FORMATS

Digital files can be saved in a number of file formats that will allow them to be moved between different types of imaging and page layout applications. These file formats also allow imagery to be cross platformed.

**EPS or .eps (Encapsulated PostScript):** Used for placing images or graphics in documents created in word processing, page layout, or drawing programs. Supports both rastered and vectored data. EPS files can be cross platformed, cropped, or edited.

**GIF or .gif (Graphics Interchange Format):** An 8-bit, low-memory option for posting images online. GIF images are limited to 256 colors, making them unsuitable for most print applications. However, their limited color quality makes them ideally suited for the limited color display range of computer monitors. GIFs are well-suited for images containing large, flat areas of one color and are often used for graphics such as logos and line art.

**JPEG or .jpg:** File format designated by the Joint Photographic Experts Group for image compression. Because it is a "lossy" compression format, image quality is sacrificed to conserve disk space. JPEGs are frequently used for placing imagery in websites and online applications where high resolution files aren't necessary. JPEGs work best for photographs, illustrations, and other complex imagery

**PDF or .pdf (Portable Document Format):** Used for allowing documents to be viewed and printed independent of the application used to create them. Often used for transferring printed pages over the web, either for downloading existing publications or for sending documents to service bureaus or commercial printers for output.

**TIFF or .tif (Tagged Image File Format):** Used for placing images or graphics in documents created in word processing, page layout, or drawing programs. Supports rasterized data and converts vectored images to bits. TIFF files can be cropped or edited. Similar to EPS, but smaller file size saves memory over EPS format.

## PHOTOGRAPHIC OPTIONS

There are various alternatives from which to choose when finding, commissioning, or otherwise producing photographic imagery. Each imaging option has its own advantages and disadvantages:

### SLIDES AND TRANSPARENCIES

| Advantages | Disadvantages |
| --- | --- |
| Slides shot with a 35 mm camera and other transparencies offer excellent color reproduction because they offer greater tonal range than color photographic prints. A good-quality transparency can be enlarged up to around seven times its size or 700%. | Slides and transparencies need to be scanned or digitized to be brought into computerized design and production. |

# PHOTOGRAPHIC OPTIONS (CONT.)

## DIGITAL PHOTOS

| Advantages | Disadvantages |
| --- | --- |
| Digital photographs can quickly be incorporated into the digital production process. | Image quality depends on the quality of the camera. Inexpensive digital cameras tend to produce unreliable results, particularly where detail and color are concerned. |

## PHOTOGRAPHIC PRINTS

| Advantages | Disadvantages |
| --- | --- |
| Color and black-and-white prints can be easily examined and evaluated for quality. Because the tonal range in a print is already compressed, they're easier to match on press. | Photographic prints can't be enlarged much from their original size without losing clarity. They must be scanned or digitized to be brought into computerized design and production. |

## STANDARD CAMERA FORMATS AND SIZES

Photographic transparencies come in a variety of sizes. In addition to the sizes most commonly used, shown on this template, larger sizes such as 8" × 10" (20.32 × 25.4 cm) are also available.

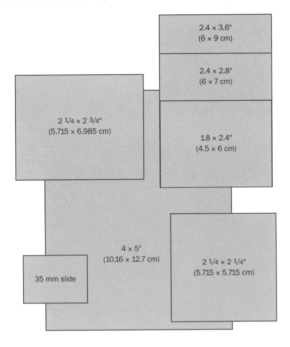

Refer to this template when determining the size of a slide or transparency. (Note: template is shown at half scale.)

## HALFTONE SCREENS

The halftone screens that are used to convert a continuous-tone image to one that can be printed come in a variety of densities measured by lines per inch (lpi), a term the industry uses for referring to the size of a screen's halftone dot. High screen rulings of 175 or 200 lpi have more halftone dots per inch and, therefore, smaller dots. Low screen rulings such as 65 or 85 lpi have larger dots. The size of a halftone dot can affect an image's quality. Those with a high lpi show more detail. However, the choice of halftone screen is often dictated by the type of paper used. Paper with a low degree of absorbency, such as coated stocks, tend to resist dot gain or the spreading of halftone dots in a halftone screen and are suitable for high lpi halftone screens. Printing images on inexpensive uncoated stocks, such as newsprint, tends to result in dot gain and requires a halftone screen with a low lpi.

Enlarged halftone screen.

Shown are some common halftone
screens as applied to the same
photograph.

65 lpi screen.

100 lpi screen.

150 lpi screen.

200 lpi screen.

## Tint Values for Halftone Screens

Screen rulings affect the perception of a screen tint as well as how overprints and reverses are perceived against the tints. Consult the chart to the right to get an idea of how a reverse or overprint will look against a screened background.

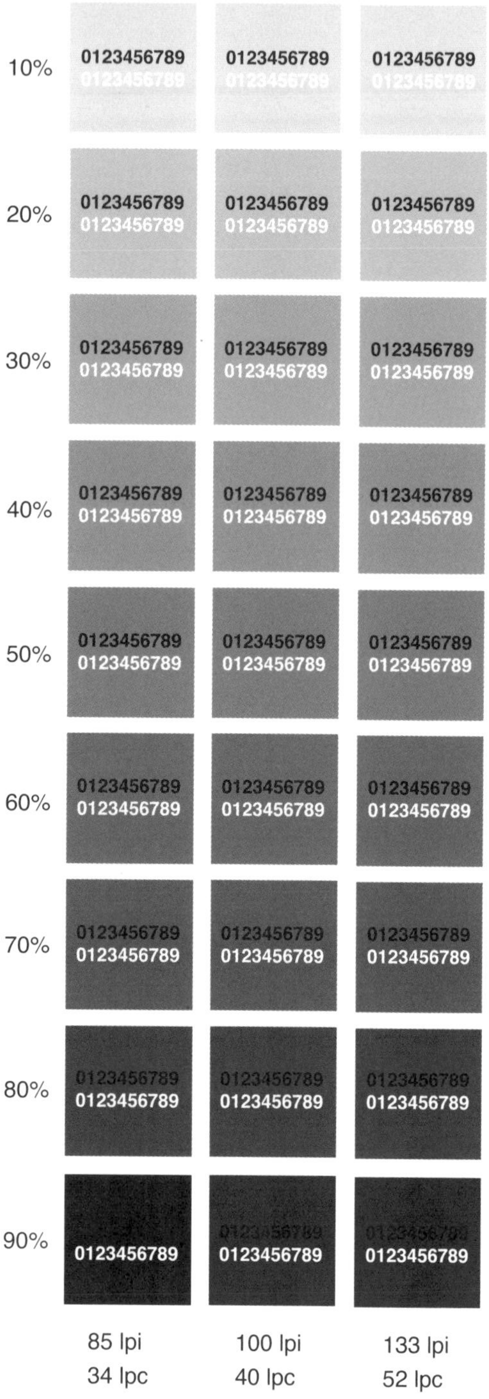

| | 85 lpi / 34 lpc | 100 lpi / 40 lpc | 133 lpi / 52 lpc |
|---|---|---|---|
| 10% | 0123456789 0123456789 | 0123456789 0123456789 | 0123456789 0123456789 |
| 20% | 0123456789 0123456789 | 0123456789 0123456789 | 0123456789 0123456789 |
| 30% | 0123456789 0123456789 | 0123456789 0123456789 | 0123456789 0123456789 |
| 40% | 0123456789 0123456789 | 0123456789 0123456789 | 0123456789 0123456789 |
| 50% | 0123456789 0123456789 | 0123456789 0123456789 | 0123456789 0123456789 |
| 60% | 0123456789 0123456789 | 0123456789 0123456789 | 0123456789 0123456789 |
| 70% | 0123456789 0123456789 | 0123456789 0123456789 | 0123456789 0123456789 |
| 80% | 0123456789 0123456789 | 0123456789 0123456789 | 0123456789 0123456789 |
| 90% | 0123456789 | 0123456789 | 0123456789 |

## DUOTONES

A duotone is a halftone printed in two colors, usually black and a second color. One plate is made for the black, picking up the highlights and shadow areas; a second plate is made for the second color, picking up the middle tones. When combined, the two plates produce a monochromatic reproduction with a full range of tones.

Red impression.

Black impression.

Duotone printed in red and black.

## Finding the Best Scanning Resolution

When you select a dpi for an image scan, you are designating the amount of image informa-tion your scanner will capture—the higher the dpi, the more image data, or potential for clar-ity your image file will have. Although scanning at a high dpi may ensure that every detail of your image will be captured, the large size of high-resolution image files makes them cum-bersome to work with. Scanning at optimum resolution means getting the best image clarity and reproduction you can achieve with the lowest possible file size or dpi.

When deciding on what scanning resolution will work best for an image, start with your image output in mind:

- *Digital display* — Anything that will be displayed on a computer monitor or as part of a digital presentation (PowerPoint, etc.) should be scanned at 72 dpi. This is the best image reproduction you can achieve, because a computer monitor's resolution is just 72 dpi.

- *Print output for studio printers* — Scanning for print reproduction depends on your output device. A 300 dpi studio printer requires images scanned at 300 dpi for optimum clarity. Let this 300 dpi rule of thumb be your guide when scan-ning line art and continuous-tone imagery for studio output.

- *Print output for commercial printers* — The scanning resolution for a continuous tone image such as photograph or illus-tration that will be converted to a halftone should be dictated by the lpi of your halftone screen. When scanning for halftone output, the scanning resolution for your image should be a dpi that is double the lpi of your line screen. For instance, a photograph reproduced with a 150 lpi halftone screen (standard for a magazine) should be scanned at 300 dpi. However, if the same photograph appears in a newspaper (where halftone screens are generally 85 lpi), the scan-ning dpi should be 170 dpi.

## Scaling an Image

Beyond output, the other consideration to keep in mind when scanning an image is scale. Reflective art that is reduced will gain clarity, whereas, reflective art that is enlarged will lose it. For instance, when a 300 dpi scanned image is enlarged by 200% (double its origi-nal size), its image resolution is reduced to 150 dpi. If the same image is reduced by 50%, its resolution becomes 600 dpi. It's best to scale your image to a size that is close to the size it will appear in its final destination, and then pick the appropriate dpi.

**When scaling an image, use this formula to arrive at the right percentage:**

Size of your reduction or enlargement × 100 ÷ the size of your original = percentage.

Example: 8" image scaled to 4" ( 4 × 100 = 400 ÷ 8 = 50% )

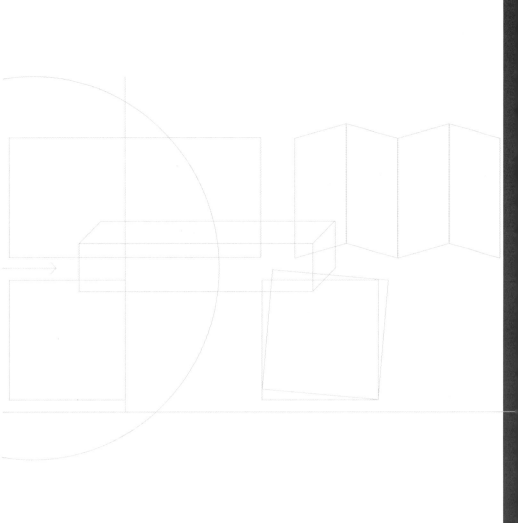

# ○ Chapter 5: Type

## TYPE BASICS AND TERMINOLOGY

Because type is measured and described in a language that is unique to the printed word, it is important to recognize and understand basic typographic terms.

*Typeface:* The design of a single set of letterforms, numerals, and punctuation marks unified by consistent visual properties. Typeface designs are identified by name, such as Arial or Palantino.

*Type style:* Modifications in a typeface that create design variety while maintaining the visual character of the typeface. These include variations in weight (light, medium, book, bold, heavy, and black), width (condensed or extended) or angle (italic or oblique vs. roman or upright).

*Type family:* A range of style variations based on a single typeface. Style attributes of type families can contain a number of modifications but will always retain a distinct visual continuity.

*Type font:* A complete set of letterforms (uppercase and lowercase), numerals and punctuation marks in a particular typeface that allows for typesetting by keystroke on a computer or other means of typographic composition.

*Letterform:* The particular style and form of each individual letter in an alphabet.

*Character:* Individual letterforms, numerals, punctuation marks, or other units that are part of a font.

*Uppercase:* The capital or larger letters of a type font (A, B, C, etc.).

*Lowercase:* Smaller letters, as opposed to capital letters (a, b, c, etc.).

### Categorizing Typefaces

There are many ways of classifying typefaces, however one of the most obvious is to separate typefaces into one of two categories based on their legibility. Because those who manufacture and work with type make this distinction, typefaces are generally broken down into *text* and *display* classifications.

# Arial Condensed Light

# Arial Regular

# **Arial Bold**

# *Arial Bold Italic*

# **Arial Black**

The type family of Arial is composed of style variations on the Arial design that include a variety of weights.

Cap height — Uppercase letter — Ascender
Serif — x height
Lowercase letter — Baseline
Bowl — Loop — Counter — Descender

A knowledge of letterform anatomy is essential to understanding how typefaces differ and distinguishing one typeface from another.

*Text typefaces* are highly legible and used mostly for large areas of text.

# Times
# Arial
Garamond

Text typefaces such as Times, Arial, and Garamond have a more traditional look and are easy on the eye. They work well for long passages of text.

*Display typefaces* are more decorative and not as legible. They tend to catch attention and/or convey a mood or attitude. They are mostly used for single or grouped words such as logotypes, headlines, or phrases.

**Impact**

Old English

Suburban

Display typefaces such as Impact, Old English, and Suburban are more expressive than text typefaces but are not suitable for large bodies of text.

## Serif and Sans Serif

Graphic arts professionals have devised other ways of organizing typefaces. A major distinction is the difference between serif and sans serif typefaces.

## Serif

Serif typefaces originated with the Romans who identified their stone shrines and public buildings with chisel-cut letterforms. To hide the ragged ends of these letterforms, the Romans would cut a short, extra stroke on the ends of their letters. This extra cut was called a serif.

## Sans serif

Sans serif typefaces were born out of the Industrial Revolution to reflect a more modern aesthetic. They are characterized by no serifs and a smooth, streamlined look.

Serif typefaces can be further broken down into subcategories that make distinctions between the types of serifs they display and their letter stroke style.

Typefaces that resemble handwriting or hand lettering fall into a category called *script*.

Old Style Roman typefaces are styled after classic Roman inscriptions. They have splayed stems, wedge-shaped serifs, and bracketed serifs.

Modern Roman typefaces show an extreme contrast between thick and thin strokes, with sharp, thin serifs.

Transitional Roman typefaces fall in between Old Style and Modern serif typefaces and exhibit characteristics of both.

Egyptian or Slab Serif typefaces have square serifs and even strokes with no thick and thin contrast. (Alternative term: Square Serif.)

All other typefaces fall into a category called *decorative*. These typefaces are highly stylized and suitable only for display purposes.

The script category of typefaces includes a variety of looks ranging from typefaces that resemble crude brush-painted signage to those that mimic the calligraphic look of pen and ink.

Decorative typefaces, such as the ones shown here, include period and novelty looks. They are most often used to attract attention and convey a mood.

## Measuring Type

Type is measured by *points*, a unit for measuring the height of type and vertical distance between lines of type. A point measures .0138 of an inch or 3.515 mm. There are 72.27 points in an inch and 28.453 points in a millimeter.

8 point

10 point

18 point

24 point

36 point

48 point

60 point

72 point

The point system of measuring type goes back to the days of metal type when sizes were classified according to the metal slug that held each character.

The amount of space between lines of type, called *leading*, is also measured in points. The term is derived from metal type where strips of lead were inserted between lines of type. (Alternative terms: line spacing, interline spacing.)

Type size: 21 points
Leading: 24 points

Type can be timeless or trendy. It can express a mood or an attitude. It can function as shape or line in a composition, or as pattern or texture.

Line length: 28 picas

Leading is typically one to two points more than the point size of a typeface. This allowance between lines provides enough space to accommodate the height of uppercase characters and ascenders as well as characters with decenders that fall below the baseline.

The horizontal length of a line of type, or its *line length*, is traditionally measured in picas, but can also be measured in inches or millimeters. There are 6.0230 picas in 1 inch and 2.371 millimeters in a pica.

The distance between characters in a word or number and between words and punctuation in a line of type is called *letterspacing*. (Alternative terms: tracking or kerning.)

# LETTER

# LETTER

Adding letterspacing to a word gives it a different aesthetic that may add design value in single or limited word applications. However, lack of legibility makes this technique inappropriate for lengthy amounts of text.

This guide includes alphabetical listings of typefaces and specimens. It is divided into two sections. The first section is limited to single-word representations, by name of display typefaces. The typefaces are organized according to whether they are decorative, scripts, or period looks. The text typeface section includes alphabets and numbers for many of the style variations that are available for each typeface.

*Note:* This guide is intended as a reference source and not as a font catalog. Check with your font supplier for additional information on style variations and font availability.

**Type Specimens: Display Typefaces**
Use this guide to identify typefaces that you're trying to match or when considering typefaces for possible use.

Decorative

**Aachen**
**Alternate Gothic**
Americana
**Aquarius**
**BALLOON**
City
**Dom Casual**
Friz Quadrata
**Hobo**
**Impact**
**MACHINE**
Modula
**Octopus**
Old English Text
Peignot
Russell Square
Sand
**STENCIL**
Suburban
Tekton
University
**Windsor**

Scripts

*Brush*
*Commercial Script*
*Gillies Gothic Bold*
*Mistral*
*Murray Hill*
*Park Avenue*
*Zapf Chancery*

Period Looks

Bauhaus
**Broadway**
BUSORAMA
**DAVIDA**
Playbill
PREMIER

The stylistic characteristics of decorative and display fonts make it relatively easy to differentiate between these typefaces. However, identifying typefaces within the text category can be more difficult. Looking for subtle differences is often the only way of differentiating one typeface from the next. Here are some guidelines to follow when trying to identify a typeface.

At first glance, these typefaces seem as though they could be the same font, particularly if you compare the uppercase "A's" on the samples set in Arial and Avant Garde. However, there are subtle differences:

- Looking at the x-height of a typeface can often help to identify it. The x-height of the letters in the Futura sample is smaller than those in the Arial and Avant Garde samples.

- The lowercase "a" can differ from one typeface to the next, as it does when comparing the sample set in Arial to those set in Avant Garde and Futura. When trying to identify a typeface, looking at the lowercase "a" will often help determine if there is a match.

Like the sans serif examples here, these serif typefaces all appear similar when you compare the uppercase "A's." The differences in these fonts can be discerned by making some comparisons.

- The x-height of the letters in the Times New Roman sample is smaller than those in the Palatino and Georgia samples.

- When comparing serif typefaces, comparing the style of the serifs can help identify a font. The Palatino and Times New Roman samples have bracketed serifs, whereas the Georgia sample does not. Bracketed serifs are slightly flared out where they join the letter.

- Comparing lowercase letterforms, especially "g's" and "f's," is a good way to note subtle differences. Notice how the loop on the "g's" descender differs between typefaces as well as the form of the letter "f."

Arial

A Hamburger fonts

Avant Garde

A Hamburger fonts

Futura

A Hamburger fonts

Palatino

A Hamburger fonts

Georgia

A Hamburger fonts

Times New Roman

A Hamburger fonts

The typefaces in this section include many of the style variations that are part of each typeface family. However, due to space limitations, condensed, extended, italic, and oblique versions have been limited to the Roman, book, or medium weight of each typeface. Condensed and extended versions of each typeface have also been restricted to one sample.

American Typewriter
ABCDEFGHIJKLMNOPQRSTUVWXYZabcdefghijklmnopq rstuvwxyz1234567890

American Typewriter Light
ABCDEFGHIJKLMNOPQRSTUVWXYZabcdefghijklmnopqr stuvwxyz1234567890

American Typewriter Bold
**ABCDEFGHIJKLMNOPQRSTUVWXYZabcdefghijklmno pqrstuvwxyz1234567890**

American Typewriter Condensed
ABCDEFGHIJKLMNOPQRSTUVWXYZabcdefghijklmnopqrstuvwxyz 1234567890

Americana
ABCDEFGHIJKLMNOPQRSTUVWXYZabcdefghijklmnop qrstuvwxyz1234567890

Americana Italic
ABCDEFGHIJKLMNOPQRSTUVWXYZabcdefghijklmnopq rstuvwxyz1234567890

Americana Bold
ABCDEFGHIJKLMNOPQRSTUVWXYZabcdefghijklmnop qrstuvwxyz1234567890

Avenir Light
ABCDEFGHIJKLMNOPQRSTUVWXYZabcdefghijklmnopqrstuvw xyz1234567890

Avenir Regular
ABCDEFGHIJKLMNOPQRSTUVWXYZabcdefghijklmnopqrstuv wxyz1234567890

Avenir Regular Oblique

*ABCDEFGHIJKLMNOPQRSTUVWXYZabcdefghijklmnopqrstuv wxyz1234567890*

Avenir Book

ABCDEFGHIJKLMNOPQRSTUVWXYZabcdefghijklmnopqrstuv wxyz1234567890

Avenir Medium

ABCDEFGHIJKLMNOPQRSTUVWXYZabcdefghijklmnopqrstuv wxyz1234567890

Avenir Medium Oblique

*ABCDEFGHIJKLMNOPQRSTUVWXYZabcdefghijklmnopqrstuv wxyz1234567890*

Avenir Black

**ABCDEFGHIJKLMNOPQRSTUVWXYZabcdefghijklmnopqrst uvwxyz1234567890**

Bauer Bodoni Roman

ABCDEFGHIJKLMNOPQRSTUVWXYZ ABCDEFGHIJKLMNOPQRSTUV WXYZ1234567890

Bauer Bodoni Italic

*ABCDEFGHIJKLMNOPQRSTUVWXYZabcdefghijklmnopqrstuvwx yz1234567890*

Bauer Bodoni Bold

**ABCDEFGHIJKLMNOPQRSTUVWXYZabcdefghijklmnopqrs tuvwxyz1234567890**

Bauer Bodoni Black

**ABCDEFGHIJKLMNOPQRSTUVWXYZabcdefghijklmnopqr stuvwxyz1234567890**

Bauer Bodoni Bold Condensed

**ABCDEFGHIJKLMNOPQRSTUVWXYZabcedfghijklmnopqrstuvwxyz 1234567890**

Bauer Bodoni Black Condensed

**ABCDEFGHIJKLMNOPQRSTUVWXYZabcdefghijklmnopqrstuvwxyz 1234567890**

Bembo Roman

ABCDEFGHIJKLMNOPQRSTUVWXYZabcdefghijklmnopqrstuvw
xyz1234567890

Bembo Italic

*ABCDEFGHIJKLMNOPQRSTUVWXYZabcdefghijklmnopqrstuvwxyz*
*1234567890*

Bembo Bold

**ABCDEFGHIJKLMNOPQRSTUVWXYZabcdefghijklmnopqrs**
**tuvwxyz1234567890**

Bembo Semibold

ABCDEFGHIJKLMNOPQRSTUVWXYZabcdefghijklmnopqrstu
vwxyz1234567890

Bembo Extra Bold

**ABCDEFGHIJKLMNOPQRSTUVWXYZabcdefghijklmnop**
**qrstuvwxyz1234567890**

ITC Benguiat Book

ABCDEFGHIJKLMNOPQRSTUVWXYZabcdefghijklmnopqrstu
vwxyz1234567890

ITC Benguiat Gothic Bold

**ABCDEFGHIJKLMNOPQRSTUVWXYZabcdefghijklmnopqrs**
**tuvwxyz1234567890**

ITC Berkeley Oldstyle Book

ABCDEFGHIJKLMNOPQRSTUVWXYZabcdefghijklmnopqrstuvwxyz
1234567890

ITC Berkeley Oldstyle Bold

**ABCDEFGHIJKLMNOPQRSTUVWXYZabcdefghijklmnopqrstuvwxyz**
**1234567890**

ITC Bodoni Book

ABCDEFGHIJKLMNOPQRSTUVWXYZabcdefghijklmnopqrstuvwxyz
1234567890

ITC Bodoni Book Italic

*ABCDEFGHIJKLMNOPQRSTUVWXYZabcdefghijklmnopqrstuvwxyz*
*1234567890*

ITC Bodoni Bold

ABCDEFGHIJKLMNOPQRSTUVWXYZabcdefghijklmnopqrstu vwxyz1234567890

ITC Bookman Roman

ABCDEFGHIJKLMNOPQRSTUVWXYZabcdefghijklmnopqr stuvwxyz1234567890

ITC Bookman Italic

*ABCDEFGHIJKLMNOPQRSTUVWXYZabcdefghijklmnopqrst uvwxyz1234567890*

ITC Bookman Bold

**ABCDEFGHIJKLMNOPQRSTUVWXYZabcdefghijklmnopqr stuvwxyz1234567890**

Century Old Style Roman

ABCDEFGHIJKLMNOPQRSTUVWXYZabcdefghijklmnopqrstuv wxyz1234567890

Century Old Style Italic

*ABCDEFGHIJKLMNOPQRSTUVWXYZabcdefghijklmnopqrstuvwx yz1234567890*

Century Old Style Bold

**ABCDEFGHIJKLMNOPQRSTUVWXYZabcdefghijklmnopqr stuvwxyz1234567890**

New Century Schoolbook Roman

ABCDEFGHIJKLMNOPQRSTUVWXYZabcdefghijklmnopqr stuvwxyz1234567890

New Century Schoolbook Italic

*ABCDEFGHIJKLMNOPQRSTUVWXYZabcdefghijklmnopqr stuvwxyz1234567890*

New Century Schoolbook Bold

**ABCDEFGHIJKLMNOPQRSTUVWXYZabcdefghijklmn opqrstuvwxyz1234567890**

Cheltenham Roman

ABCDEFGHIJKLMNOPQRSTUVWXYZabcdefghijklmnopqrstuv
wxyz1234567890

Cheltenham Italic

ABCDEFGHIJKLMNOPQRSTUVWXYZabcdefghijklmnopqrstuvwxyz
1234567890

Cheltenham Bold

**ABCDEFGHIJKLMNOPQRSTUVWXYZabcdefghijklmnopqrst
uvwxyz1234567890**

Clarendon Light

ABCDEFGHIJKLMNOPQRSTUVWXYZabcdefghijklmnopq
rstuvwxyz1234567890

Clarendon Roman

ABCDEFGHIJKLMNOPQRSTUVWXYZabcdefghijklmnopq
rstuvwxyz1234567890

Clarendon Bold

**ABCDEFGHIJKLMNOPQRSTUVWXYZabcdefghijklmnop
qrstuvwxyz1234567890**

Clearface Roman

ABCDEFGHIJKLMNOPQRSTUVWXYZabcdefghijklmnopqrstuvwxyz
1234567890

Clearface Italic

ABCDEFGHIJKLMNOPQRSTUVWXYZabcdefghijklmnopqrstuvwxyz
1234567890

Clearface Bold

ABCDEFGHIJKLMNOPQRSTUVWXYZabcdefghijklmnopqrstuvwxyz
1234567890

Clearface Heavy

**ABCDEFGHIJKLMNOPQRSTUVWXYZabcdefghijklmnopqrstuvwxyz
1234567890**

Clearface Black

**ABCDEFGHIJKLMNOPQRSTUVWXYZabcdefghijklmnopqrstu
vwxyz1234567890**

ITC Galliard Roman

ABCDEFGHIJKLMNOPQRSTUVWXYZabcdefghijklmnopqrstu
vwxyz1234567890

ITC Galliard Italic

*ABCDEFGHIJKLMNOPQRSTUVWXYZabcdefghijklmnopqrstuv
wxyz1234567890*

ITC Galliard Bold

**ABCDEFGHIJKLMNOPQRSTUVWXYZabcdefghijklmnopq
rstuvwxyz1234567890**

ITC Galliard Black

**ABCDEFGHIJKLMNOPQRSTUVWXYZabcdefghijklmnop
qrstuvwxyz1234567890**

ITC Galliard Ultra

**ABCDEFGHIJKLMNOPQRSTUVWXYZabcdefghijklmno
pqrstuvwxyz1234567890**


ITC Garamond Light

ABCDEFGHIJKLMNOPQRSTUVWXYZabcdefghijklmnopqrstuvwxyz
1234567890

ITC Garamond Light Italic

*ABCDEFGHIJKLMNOPQRSTUVWXYZabcedfghijklmnopqrstuvwxyz
1234567890*

ITC Garamond Book

ABCDEFGHIJKLMNOPQRSTUVWXYZabcdefghijklmnopqrstuvwxyz
1234567890

ITC Garamond Bold

**ABCDEFGHIJKLMNOPQRSTUVWXYZabcdefghijklmnopqrstu
vwxyz1234567890**

ITC Garamond Ultra

**ABCDEFGHIJKLMNOPQRSTUVWXYZabcdefghijklmnopq
rstuvwxyz1234567890**

ITC Garamond Light Condensed

ABCDEFGHIJKLMNOPQRSTUVWXYZabcdefghijklmnopqrstuvwxyz1234567890

ITC Garamond Book Condensed

ABCDEFGHIJKLMNOPQRSTUVWXYZabcdefghijklmnopqrstuvwxyz1234567890

ITC Garamond Bold Condensed

**ABCDEFGHIJKLMNOPQRSTUVWXYZabcdefghijklmnopqrstuvwxyz
1234567890**

ITC Garamond Ultra Condensed
**ABCDEFGHIJKLMNOPQRSTUVWXYZabcdefghijklmnopqrstuvwxyz
1234567890**

Glypha 35 Thin
ABCDEFGHIJKLMNOPQRSTUVWXYZabcdefghijklmnopqrstuvwxyz
1234567890

Glypha 45 Light
ABCDEFGHIJKLMNOPQRSTUVWXYZabcdefghijklmnopqrstuvwxyz
1234567890

Glypha 55 Regular
ABCDEFGHIJKLMNOPQRSTUVWXYZabcdefghijklmnopqrs
tuvwxyz1234567890

Glypha 55 Oblique
*ABCDEFGHIJKLMNOPQRSTUVWXYZabcdefghijklmnopqrs
tuvwxyz1234567890*

Glypha 65 Bold
**ABCDEFGHIJKLMNOPQRSTUVWXYZabcdefghijklmnopqr
stuvwxyz1234567890**

Glypha 75 Black
**ABCDEFGHIJKLMNOPQRSTUVWXYZabcdefghijklmnopq
rstuvwxyz1234567890**

Italia Book
ABCDEFGHIJKLMNOPQRSTUVWXYZabcdefghijklmnopqrstuvwxyz
1234567890

Italia Medium
**ABCDEFGHIJKLMNOPQRSTUVWXYZabcdefghijklmnopqrstuvwx
yz1234567890**

Italia Bold
**ABCDEFGHIJKLMNOPQRSTUVWXYZabcdefghijklmnopqrstuvw
xyz1234567890**

Janson Text Roman
ABCDEFGHIJKLMNOPQRSTUVWXYZabcdefghijklmnopqrst
uvwxyz1234567890

Janson Text Italic

*ABCDEFGHIJKLMNOPQRSTUVWXYZabcdefghijklmnopqrstuvwxyz 1234567890*

Janson Text Bold

**ABCDEFGHIJKLMNOPQRSTUVWXYZabcdefghijklmnopq rstuvwxyz1234567890**

ITC Korinna Regular

ABCDEFGHIJKLMNOPQRSTUVWXYZabcdefghijklmnopqrstu vwxyz1234567890

ITC Korinna Kursiv

*ABCDEFGHIJKLMNOPQRSTUVWXYZabcdefghijklmnopqrstuv wxyz1234567890*

ITC Korinna Bold

**ABCDEFGHIJKLMNOPQRSTUVWXYZabcdefghijklmnopqrst uvwxyz1234567890**

ITC Lubalin Graph Book

ABCDEFGHIJKLMNOPQRSTUVWXYZabcdefghijklmnopqrst uvwxyz1234567890

ITC Lubalin Graph Demi

**ABCDEFGHIJKLMNOPQRSTUVWXYZabcdefghijklmnopqrs tuvwxyz1234567890**

Melior Roman

ABCDEFGHIJKLMNOPQRSTUVWXYZabcdefghijklmnopqrstu vwxyz1234567890

Melior Italic

*ABCDEFGHIJKLMNOPQRSTUVWXYZabcdefghijklmnopqrstu vwxyz1234567890*

Melior Bold

**ABCDEFGHIJKLMNOPQRSTUVWXYZabcdefghijklmnopqrst uvwxyz1234567890**

Memphis Light

ABCDEFGHIJKLMNOPQRSTUVWXYZabcdefghijklmnopqrstuv wxyz1234567890

Memphis Medium

ABCDEFGHIJKLMNOPQRSTUVWXYZabcdefghijklmnopqrst
uvwxyz1234567890

Memphis Medium Italic

*ABCDEFGHIJKLMNOPQRSTUVWXYZabcdefghijklmnopqrstu
vwxyz1234567890*

Memphis Bold

**ABCDEFGHIJKLMNOPQRSTUVWXYZabcdefghijklmnopqrst
uvwxyz1234567890**

Memphis Extra Bold

**ABCDEFGHIJKLMNOPQRSTUVWXYZabcdefghijk
lmnopqrstuvwxyz1234567890**

Minion Roman

ABCDEFGHIJKLMNOPQRSTUVWXYZabcdefghijklmnopqrstuvwxyz
1234567890

Minion Italic

*ABCDEFGHIJKLMNOPQRSTUVWXYZabcdefghijklmnopqrstuvwxyz
1234567890*

Minion Semibold

ABCDEFGHIJKLMNOPQRSTUVWXYZabcdefghijklmnopqrstuvwx
yz1234567890

Minion Bold

**ABCDEFGHIJKLMNOPQRSTUVWXYZabcdefghijklmnopqrstuvwx
yz1234567890**

Minion Black

**ABCDEFGHIJKLMNOPQRSTUVWXYZabcdefghijklmnopqrstuvw
xyz1234567890**


ITC New Baskerville Roman

ABCDEFGHIJKLMNOPQRSTUVWXYZabcdefghijklmnopqrstuv
wxyz1234567890

ITC New Baskerville Italic

*ABCDEFGHIJKLMNOPQRSTUVWXYZabcdefghijklmnopqrstuvwxyz
1234567890*

ITC New Baskerville Bold

**ABCDEFGHIJKLMNOPQRSTUVWXYZabcdefghijklmnopqrstuv
wxyz1234567890**

Palatino Roman

ABCDEFGHIJKLMNOPQRSTUVWXYZabcdefghijklmnopqrstu vwxyz1234567890

Palatino Italic

*ABCDEFGHIJKLMNOPQRSTUVWXYZabcdefghijklmnopqrstuvw xyz1234567890*

Palatino Bold

**ABCDEFGHIJKLMNOPQRSTUVWXYZabcdefghijklmnopqr stuvwxyz1234567890**

Plantin Light

ABCDEFGHIJKLMNOPQRSTUVWXYZabcdefghijklmnopqrs tuvwxyz1234567890

Plantin Roman

ABCDEFGHIJKLMNOPQRSTUVWXYZabcdefghijklmnopqrs tuvwxyz1234567890

Plantin Semibold

ABCDEFGHIJKLMNOPQRSTUVWXYZabcdefghijklmnop qrstuvwxyz1234567890

Plantin Bold Condensed

**ABCDEFGHIJKLMNOPQRSTUVWXYZabcdefghijklmnopqrstuvwxyz1234 567890**

Poster Bodoni

**ABCDEFGHIJKLMNOPQRSTUVWXYZabcdefghijkl mnopqrstuvwxyz1234567890**

Poster Bodoni Italic

***ABCDEFGHIJKLMNOPQRSTUVWXYZabcdefghijkl mnopqrstuvwxyz1234567890***

Rockwell Light

ABCDEFGHIJKLMNOPQRSTUVWXYZabcdefghijklmnopqrstuvwxyz 1234567890

Rockwell Regular

ABCDEFGHIJKLMNOPQRSTUVWXYZabcdefghijklmnopqrstuv wxyz1234567890

Rockwell Italic

ABCDEFGHIJKLMNOPQRSTUVWXYZabcdefghijklmnopqrstuvw
xyz1234567890

Rockwell Bold

**ABCDEFGHIJKLMNOPQRSTUVWXYZabcdefghijklmnopq
rstuvwxyz1234567890**

Rockwell Extra Bold

**ABCDEFGHIJKLMNOPQRSTUVWXYZabcdefghijk
lmnopqrstuvwxyz1234567890**

Rockwell Condensed

ABCDEFGHIJKLMNOPQRSTUVWXYZabcdefghijklmnopqrstuvwxyz1234567890

Sabon Roman

ABCDEFGHIJKLMNOPQRSTUVWXYZabcdefghijklmnopqrstu
vwxyz1234567890

Sabon Italic

ABCDEFGHIJKLMNOPQRSTUVWXYZabcdefghijklmnopqrst
uvwxyz1234567890

Sabon Bold

**ABCDEFGHIJKLMNOPQRSTUVWXYZabcdefghijklmnopqrst
uvwxyz1234567890**

Serifa Light

ABCDEFGHIJKLMNOPQRSTUVWXYZabcdefghijklmnopqrstuvwx
yz1234567890

Serifa Roman

ABCDEFGHIJKLMNOPQRSTUVWXYZabcdefghijklmnopqrs
tuvwxyz1234567890

Serifa Italic

ABCDEFGHIJKLMNOPQRSTUVWXYZabcdefghijklmnopqrst
uvwxyz1234567890

Serifa Bold

**ABCDEFGHIJKLMNOPQRSTUVWXYZabcdefghijklmnopq
rstuvwxyz1234567890**

Serifa Black

**ABCDEFGHIJKLMNOPQRSTUVWXYZabcdefghijklmnop
qrstuvwxyz1234567890**

ITC Stone Serif Medium

ABCDEFGHIJKLMNOPQRSTUVWXYZabcdefghijklmnopqrstu
vwxyz1234567890

ITC Stone Serif Medium Italic

*ABCDEFGHIJKLMNOPQRSTUVWXYZabcdefghijklmnopqrstuvwx
yz1234567890*

ITC Stone Serif Semibold

**ABCDEFGHIJKLMNOPQRSTUVWXYZabcdefghijklmnopqrs
tuvwxyz1234567890**

ITC Stone Serif Bold

**ABCDEFGHIJKLMNOPQRSTUVWXYZabcdefghijklmn
opqrstuvwxyz1234567890**

Times Roman

ABCDEFGHIJKLMNOPQRSTUVWXYZabcdefghijklmnopqrstuvwxyz
1234567890

Times Italic

*ABCDEFGHIJKLMNOPQRSTUVWXYZabcdefghijklmnopqrstuvwxyz
1234567890*

Times Semibold

**ABCDEFGHIJKLMNOPQRSTUVWXYZabcdefghijklmnopqrstuv
wxyz1234567890**

Times Bold

**ABCDEFGHIJKLMNOPQRSTUVWXYZabcdefghijklmnopqrstuv
wxyz1234567890**

Times New Roman Regular

ABCDEFGHIJKLMNOPQRSTUVWXYZabcdefghijklmnopqrstuvwxyz
1234567890

Times New Roman Italic

*ABCDEFGHIJKLMNOPQRSTUVWXYZabcdefghijklmnopqrstuvwxyz
1234567890*

Times New Roman Bold

**ABCDEFGHIJKLMNOPQRSTUVWXYZabcdefghijklmnopqrstuv
wxyz1234567890**

ITC Weideman Book

ABCDEFGHIJKLMNOPQRSTUVWXYZabcdefghijklmnopqrstuvwxyz
1234567890

ITC Weideman Book Italic

ABCDEFGHIJKLMNOPQRSTUVWXYZabcdefghijklmnopqrstuvwxyz
1234567890

ITC Weideman Medium

**ABCDEFGHIJKLMNOPQRSTUVWXYZabcdefghijklmnopqrstuvwxyz
1234567890**

ITC Weideman Bold

**ABCDEFGHIJKLMNOPQRSTUVWXYZabcdefghijklmnopqrstuvwxyz
1234567890**


SANS SERIF

Akzidenz-Grotesque

ABCDEFGHIJKLMNOPQRSTUVWXYZabcdefghijklmnopqrstuvw
xyz1234567890

Akzidenz-Grotesque Light

ABCDEFGHIJKLMNOPQRSTUVWXYZabcdefghijklmnopqrstuvwxyz
1234567890

Akzidenz-Grotesque Bold

**ABCDEFGHIJKLMNOPQRSTUVWXYZabcdefghijklmnopqrstuvw
xyz1234567890**

Akzidenz-Grotesque Black

**ABCDEFGHIJKLMNOPQRSTUVWXYZabcdefghijklmnopqr
stuvwxyz1234567890**


Antique Olive Light

ABCDEFGHIJKLMNOPQRSTUVWXYZabcdefghijklmnopqrstuvwx
yz1234567890

Antique Olive Roman

**ABCDEFGHIJKLMNOPQRSTUVWXYZabcdefghijklmnopqrst
uvwxyz1234567890**

Antique Olive Bold

**ABCDEFGHIJKLMNOPQRSTUVWXYZabcdefghijklmnopqrs
tuvwxyz1234567890**

Arial Regular
ABCDEFGHIJKLMNOPQRSTUVWXYZabcdefghijklmnopqrstuv
wxyz1234567890

Arial Light
ABCDEFGHIJKLMNOPQRSTUVWXYZabcdefghijklmnopqrstuv
wxyz1234567890

Arial Medium
**ABCDEFGHIJKLMNOPQRSTUVWXYZabcdefghijklmnopqrstu
vwxyz1234567890**

Arial Extra Bold
**ABCDEFGHIJKLMNOPQRSTUVWXYZabcdefghijklmnopq
rstuvwxyz1234567890**

Arial Condensed
ABCDEFGHIJKLMNOPQRSTUVWXYZabcdefghijklmnopqrstuvwxyz
1234567890

Arial Narrow Regular
ABCDEFGHIJKLMNOPQRSTUVWXYZabcdefghijklmnopqrstuvwxyz
1234567890

Avant Garde
ABCDEFGHIJKLMNOPQRSTUVWXYZabcdefghijklmnopqrstu
vwxyz1234567890

Avant Garde Extra Light
ABCDEFGHIJKLMNOPQRSTUVWXYZabcdefghijklmnopqrstuv
wxyz1234567890

Avant Garde Book
ABCDEFGHIJKLMNOPQRSTUVWXYZabcdefghijklmnopqrstu
vwxyz1234567890

Avant Garde Book Oblique
*ABCDEFGHIJKLMNOPQRSTUVWXYZabcdefghijklmnopqrstu
vwxyz1234567890*

Avant Garde Medium
ABCDEFGHIJKLMNOPQRSTUVWXYZabcdefghijklmnopqrstu
vwxyz1234567890

Avant Garde Demi
**ABCDEFGHIJKLMNOPQRSTUVWXYZabcdefghijklmnopqrstu
vwxyz1234567890**

Avant Garde Bold

**ABCDEFGHIJKLMNOPQRSTUVWXYZabcdefghijklmnopqr
stuvwxyz1234567890**

Avant Garde Condensed Book

ABCDEFGHIJKLMNOPQRSTUVWXYZabcdefghijklmnopqrstuvwxyz
1234567890


ITC Eras Light

ABCDEFGHIJKLMNOPQRSTUVWXYZabcdefghijklmnopqrstuvwxyz
1234567890

ITC Eras Book

ABCDEFGHIJKLMNOPQRSTUVWXYZabcdefghijklmnopqrstuvwxyz
1234567890

ITC Eras Medium

ABCDEFGHIJKLMNOPQRSTUVWXYZabcdefghijklmnopqrstuvwx
yz1234567890

ITC Eras Demi

**ABCDEFGHIJKLMNOPQRSTUVWXYZabcdefghijklmnopqrst
uvwxyz1234567890**

ITC Eras Bold

**ABCDEFGHIJKLMNOPQRSTUVWXYZabcdefghijklmnopq
rstuvwxyz1234567890**

ITC Eras Ultra

**ABCDEFGHIJKLMNOPQRSTUVWXYZabcdefghijklmn
opqrstuvwxyz1234567890**


Folio Light

ABCDEFGHIJKLMNOPQRSTUVWXYZabcdefghijklmnopqrstuvw
xyz1234567890

Folio Medium

ABCDEFGHIJKLMNOPQRSTUVWXYZabcdefghijklmnopqrstuv
wxyz1234567890

Folio Bold

**ABCDEFGHIJKLMNOPQRSTUVWXYZabcdefghijklmn
opqrstuvwxyz1234567890**

Folio Extra Bold

**ABCDEFGHIJKLMNOPQRSTUVWXYZabcdefghijklmno
pqrstuvwxyz1234567890**

Folio Bold Condensed
**ABCDEFGHIJKLMNOPQRSTUVWXYZabcdefghijklmnopqrstuvwxyz1234567890**

ITC Franklin Gothic Book
ABCDEFGHIJKLMNOPQRSTUVWXYZabcdefghijklmnopqrstuvwxyz
1234567890

ITC Franklin Gothic Book Italic
*ABCDEFGHIJKLMNOPQRSTUVWXYZabcdefghijklmnopqrstuvwxyz*
*1234567890*

ITC Franklin Gothic Demi
**ABCDEFGHIJKLMNOPQRSTUVWXYZabcdefghijklmnopqrstuvwx
yz1234567890**

ITC Franklin Gothic Heavy
**ABCDEFGHIJKLMNOPQRSTUVWXYZabcdefghijklmnopqrstu
vwxyz1234567890**

Friz Quadrata Regular
ABCDEFGHIJKLMNOPQRSTUVWXYZabcdefghijklmnopqrstuvwxyz
1234567890

Friz Quadrata Bold
**ABCDEFGHIJKLMNOPQRSTUVWXYZabcdefghijklmnopqrstuvwxyz
1234567890**

Frutiger Light
ABCDEFGHIJKLMNOPQRSTUVWXYZabcdefghijklmnopqrstuvwxyz
1234567890

Frutiger Regular
ABCDEFGHIJKLMNOPQRSTUVWXYZabcdefghijklmnopqrstuv
wxyz1234567890

Frutiger Regular Italic
*ABCDEFGHIJKLMNOPQRSTUVWXYZabcdefghijklmnopqrstuv*
*wxyz1234567890*

Frutiger Bold
**ABCDEFGHIJKLMNOPQRSTUVWXYZabcdefghijklmnopqrstuv
wxyz1234567890**

Frutiger Black
**ABCDEFGHIJKLMNOPQRSTUVWXYZabcdefghijklmnopqr
stuvwxyz1234567890**

Frutiger Ultra Black
## ABCDEFGHIJKLMNOPQRSTUVWXYZabcdefghijklm nopqrstuvwxyz1234567890

Futura Light
ABCDEFGHIJKLMNOPQRSTUVWXYZabcdefghijklmnopqrstuvwxyz 1234567890

Futura Book
ABCDEFGHIJKLMNOPQRSTUVWXYZabcdefghijklmnopqrstuvwxyz 1234567890

Futura Book Oblique
*ABCDEFGHIJKLMNOPQRSTUVWXYZabcdefghijklmnopqrstuv wxyz1234567890*

Futura Bold
**ABCDEFGHIJKLMNOPQRSTUVWXYZabcdefghijklmnop qrstuvwxyz1234567890**

Futura Heavy
**ABCDEFGHIJKLMNOPQRSTUVWXYZabcdefghijklmnopqrstuvwxyz 1234567890**

Futura Extra Bold
**ABCDEFGHIJKLMNOPQRSTUVWXYZabcdefghijklm nopqrstuvwxyz1234567890**

Futura Condensed
ABCDEFGHIJKLMNOPQRSTUVWXYZabcdefghijklmnopqrstuvwxyz1234567890

Gil Sans Light
ABCDEFGHIJKLMNOPQRSTUVWXYZabcdefghijklmnopqrstuvwxyz 1234567890

Gil Sans Regular
ABCDEFGHIJKLMNOPQRSTUVWXYZabcdefghijklmnopqrstuvwxyz 1234567890

Gil Sans Italic
*ABCDEFGHIJKLMNOPQRSTUVWXYZabcdefghijklmnopqrstuvwxyz 1234567890*

Gil Sans Bold
**ABCDEFGHIJKLMNOPQRSTUVWXYZabcdefghijklmnopqr stuvwxyz1234567890**

Gil Sans Extra Bold

**ABCDEFGHIJKLMNOPQRSTUVWXYZabcdefghijklmn opqrstuvwxyz1234567890**

Gil Sans Ultra Bold

**ABCDEFGHIJKLMNOPQRSTUVWXYZabcdefghi jklmnopqrstuvwxyz1234567890**

Helvetica Light

ABCDEFGHIJKLMNOPQRSTUVWXYZabcdefghijklmnopqrstuv wxyz1234567890

Helvetica Light Oblique

*ABCDEFGHIJKLMNOPQRSTUVWXYZabcdefghijklmnopqrstuv wxyz1234567890*

Helvetica Black

**ABCDEFGHIJKLMNOPQRSTUVWXYZabcdefghijklm nopqrstuvwxyz1234567890**

Helvetica Condensed

ABCDEFGHIJKLMNOPQRSTUVWXYZabcdefghijklmnopqrstuvwxyz 1234567890

Helvetica Compressed

ABCDEFGHIJKLMNOPQRSTUVWXYZabcdefghijklmnopqrstuvwxyz1234567890

Helvetica Rounded Bold

**ABCDEFGHIJKLMNOPQRSTUVWXYZabcdefghijklmnopqr stuvwxyz1234567890**

Helvetica Rounded Bold Oblique

*ABCDEFGHIJKLMNOPQRSTUVWXYZabcdefghijklmnopqr stuvwxyz1234567890*

Helvetica Rounded Black

**ABCDEFGHIJKLMNOPQRSTUVWXYZabcdefghijklmn opqrstuvwxyz1234567890**

Helvetica Rounded Bold Condensed

**ABCDEFGHIJKLMNOPQRSTUVWXYZabcdefghijklmnopqrstuvwxyz 1234567890**

Kabel Light

ABCDEFGHIJKLMNOPQRSTUVWXYZabcdefghijklmnopqrstuvwxyz 1234567890

Kabel Book

ABCDEFGHIJKLMNOPQRSTUVWXYZabcdefghijklmnopqrstuvwxyz
1234567890

Kabel Heavy

**ABCDEFGHIJKLMNOPQRSTUVWXYZabcdefghijklmnopqrstuvwx
yz1234567890**

Kabel Black

**ABCDEFGHIJKLMNOPQRSTUVWXYZabcdefghijklmnopqrstuvw
xyz1234567890**

Neue Helvetica Ultra Light

ABCDEFGHIJKLMNOPQRSTUVWXYZabcdefghijklmnopqrstuvwxyz
1234567890

Neue Helvetica Thin

ABCDEFGHIJKLMNOPQRSTUVWXYZabcdefghijklmnopqrstuvwxyz
1234567890

Neue Helvetica Light

ABCDEFGHIJKLMNOPQRSTUVWXYZabcdefghijklmnopqrstuvwx
yz1234567890

Neue Helvetica Medium

ABCDEFGHIJKLMNOPQRSTUVWXYZabcdefghijklmnopqrstu
vwxyz1234567890

Neue Helvetica Medium Italic

*ABCDEFGHIJKLMNOPQRSTUVWXYZabcdefghijklmnopqrstu
vwxyz1234567890*

Neue Helvetica Bold

**ABCDEFGHIJKLMNOPQRSTUVWXYZabcdefghijklmnopqrs
tuvwxyz1234567890**

Neue Helvetica Heavy

**ABCDEFGHIJKLMNOPQRSTUVWXYZabcdefghijklmnopqr
stuvwxyz1234567890**

Neue Helvetica Black

**ABCDEFGHIJKLMNOPQRSTUVWXYZabcdefghijklmnop
qrstuvwxyz1234567890**

Neue Helvetica Condensed

ABCDEFGHIJKLMNOPQRSTUVWXYZabcdefghijklmnopqrstuvwxyz1234567890

Neue Helvetica Extended

ABCDEFGHIJKLMNOPQRSTUVWXYZabcdefghijklmno pqrstuvwxyz1234567890

News Gothic Regular

ABCDEFGHIJKLMNOPQRSTUVWXYZabcdefghijklmnopqrstuvwxyz 1234567890

News Gothic Italic

ABCDEFGHIJKLMNOPQRSTUVWXYZabcdefghijklmnopqrstuvwxyz 1234567890

News Gothic Bold

**ABCDEFGHIJKLMNOPQRSTUVWXYZabcdefghijklmnopqrstuv wxyz1234567890**

Optima Regular

ABCDEFGHIJKLMNOPQRSTUVWXYZabcdefghijklmnopqrstuvw xyz1234567890

Optima Oblique

*ABCDEFGHIJKLMNOPQRSTUVWXYZabcdefghijklmnopqrstuvw xyz1234567890*

Optima Bold

**ABCDEFGHIJKLMNOPQRSTUVWXYZabcdefghijklmnopqrstuvw xyz1234567890**

Agfa Rotis Sans Serif Light

ABCDEFGHIJKLMNOPQRSTUVWXYZabcdefghijklmnopqrstuvwxyz 1234567890

Agfa Rotis Sans Serif Regular

ABCDEFGHIJKLMNOPQRSTUVWXYZabcdefghijklmnopqrstuvwxyz 1234567890

Agfa Rotis Sans Serif Italic

*ABCDEFGHIJKLMNOPQRSTUVWXYZabcdefghijklmnopqrstuvwxyz 1234567890*

Agfa Rotis Sans Serif Bold

**ABCDEFGHIJKLMNOPQRSTUVWXYZabcdefghijklmnopqrstuvwxyz 1234567890**

Agfa Rotis Sans Serif Extra Bold
**ABCDEFGHIJKLMNOPQRSTUVWXYZabcdefghijklmnopqrstuvwxyz**
**1234567890**

Agfa Rotis Semisans Light
ABCDEFGHIJKLMNOPQRSTUVWXYZabcdefghijklmnopqrstuvwxyz
1234567890

Agfa Rotis Semisans Regular
ABCDEFGHIJKLMNOPQRSTUVWXYZabcdefghijklmnopqrstuvwxyz
1234567890

Agfa Rotis Semisans Italic
*ABCDEFGHIJKLMNOPQRSTUVWXYZabcdefghijklmnopqrstuvwxyz*
*1234567890*

Agfa Rotis Semisans Bold
**ABCDEFGHIJKLMNOPQRSTUVWXYZabcdefghijklmnopqrstuvwxyz**
**1234567890**

Agfa Rotis Semisans Extra Bold
**ABCDEFGHIJKLMNOPQRSTUVWXYZabcdefghijklmnopqrstuvwxyz**
**1234567890**

ITC Stone Sans Medium
ABCDEFGHIJKLMNOPQRSTUVWXYZabcdefghijklmnopqrstuvwx
yz1234567890

ITC Stone Sans Medium Italic
*ABCDEFGHIJKLMNOPQRSTUVWXYZabcdefghijklmnopqrstuvwxyz*
*1234567890*

ITC Stone Sans Semibold
**ABCDEFGHIJKLMNOPQRSTUVWXYZabcdefghijklmnopqrstu**
**vwxyz1234567890**

ITC Stone Sans Bold
**ABCDEFGHIJKLMNOPQRSTUVWXYZabcdefghijklmnopqr**
**stuvwxyz1234567890**

ITC Symbol Book
ABCDEFGHIJKLMNOPQRSTUVWXYZabcdefghijklmnopqrstuvw
xyz1234567890

ITC Symbol Book Italic
*ABCDEFGHIJKLMNOPQRSTUVWXYZabcdefghijklmnopqrstuvwxyz*
*1234567890*

ITC Symbol Medium
ABCDEFGHIJKLMNOPQRSTUVWXYZabcdefghijklmnopqrstu
vwxyz1234567890

ITC Symbol Bold
**ABCDEFGHIJKLMNOPQRSTUVWXYZabcdefghijklmnopqrs
tuvwxyz1234567890**

ITC Symbol Black
**ABCDEFGHIJKLMNOPQRSTUVWXYZabcdefghijklmno
pqrstuvwxyz1234567890**

Trade Gothic Light
ABCDEFGHIJKLMNOPQRSTUVWXYZabcdefghijklmnopqrstuvwxyz
1234567890

Trade Gothic Regular
ABCDEFGHIJKLMNOPQRSTUVWXYZabcdefghijklmnopqrstuvwxyz
1234567890

Trade Gothic Oblique
*ABCDEFGHIJKLMNOPQRSTUVWXYZabcdefghijklmnopqrstuvwxyz*
*1234567890*

Trade Gothic Bold
**ABCDEFGHIJKLMNOPQRSTUVWXYZabcdefghijklmnopqrstuvwxyz1234
567890**

Trade Gothic Bold No. 2
**ABCDEFGHIJKLMNOPQRSTUVWXYZabcdefghijklmnopqrstuvwxyz
1234567890**

Trade Gothic Condensed
ABCDEFGHIJKLMNOPQRSTUVWXYZabcdefghijklmnopqrstuvwxyz1234567890

Univers 45 Light
ABCDEFGHIJKLMNOPQRSTUVWXYZabcdefghijklmnopqrstuv
wxyz1234567890

Univers 55

ABCDEFGHIJKLMNOPQRSTUVWXYZabcdefghijklmnopqrst uvwxyz1234567890

Univers 55 Oblique

*ABCDEFGHIJKLMNOPQRSTUVWXYZabcdefghijklmnopqrst uvwxyz1234567890*

Univers 65 Bold

**ABCDEFGHIJKLMNOPQRSTUVWXYZabcdefghijklmnopqrst uvwxyz1234567890**

Univers 75 Black

**ABCDEFGHIJKLMNOPQRSTUVWXYZabcdefghijklmn opqrstuvwxyz1234567890**

Univers 57 Condensed

ABCDEFGHIJKLMNOPQRSTUVWXYZabcdefghijklmnopqrstuvwxyz 1234567890

Univers 53 Extended

ABCDEFGHIJKLMNOPQRSTUVWXYZabcdefghij klmnopqrstuvwxyz1234567890

# ○ Chapter 6: Paper

## NORTH AMERICAN SHEET SIZES

Most paper manufactured and sold in North America is measured in inches. Sheet sizes are based on trimming a quantity of 8 1/2" × 11" items or pages from a single sheet with a minimum of waste. Some sheet sizes, such as 11" × 17", are exact multiples of the 8 1/2" × 11" inch standard. Other sheet sizes are also based on multiples of 8 1/2" × 11", but are slightly oversized to accommodate on-press requirements. For instance, a 23" × 35" inch sheet would yield sixteen trimmed 8 1/2" × 11" flyers or a sixteen-page signature while allowing a narrow margin for bleeds, grippers, and color bars.

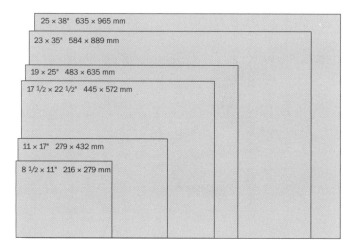

Printers in North America use sheets measured in inches with sizes based on multiples of 8 1/2" × 11" inches.

## NORTH AMERICAN SHEET SIZES AND METRIC EQUIVALENTS

| Size (inches) | Size (millimeters) |
|---|---|
| 8 1/2 × 11 | 216 × 279 |
| 11 × 17 | 279 × 432 |
| 17 1/2 × 22 1/2 | 445 × 572 |
| 19 × 25 | 483 × 635 |
| 23 × 35 | 584 × 889 |
| 25 × 38 | 635 × 965 |

## INTERNATIONAL, OR ISO, SHEET SIZES

Papers manufactured and sold outside of North America are based on 1 square meter. The International Standards Organization (ISO) system of paper sizes applies to all grades of paper and paper board and consists of five series of sizes: A, RA, SR, B, and C. Within each series, each sheet is twice the size of the next smaller sheet and half the size of the next larger sheet.

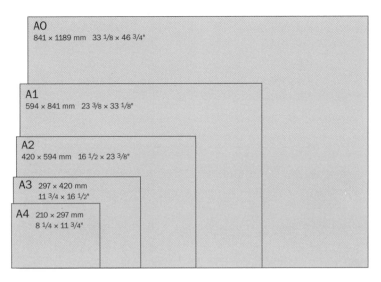

The starting point for ISO sizes is the A0 sheet, which measures 841 × 1189 mm (33 1/8" × 46 3/4") and has an area of 1 square meter. Each smaller size is a fraction of the A0 size. For instance, the A1 size (594 × 841 mm) is half of A0, and the A2 (420 × 594 mm) is one quarter of A0. Sizes larger than A0 retain the same proportions and a numeral prefix is added to the letter. For example, a 2A0 sheet is twice the size (1189 × 1682 mm) of an A0 sheet. The A series is used for general printed matter, including letterhead and publications.

## ISO A SHEET SIZES AND INCH EQUIVALENTS

| ISO Size | Size (millimeters) | Size (inches) *approx.* |
|---|---|---|
| 4A0 | 1682 × 2378 | 66 1/4 × 93 3/8 |
| 2A0 | 1189 × 1682 | 25 1/2 × 36 1/8 |
| A0 | 841 × 1189 | 33 1/8 × 46 3/4 |
| A1 | 594 × 841 | 23 3/8 × 33 1/8 |
| A2 | 420 × 594 | 16 1/2 × 23 3/8 |
| A3 | 297 × 420 | 11 3/4 × 16 1/2 |
| A4 | 210 × 297 | 8 1/4 × 11 3/4 |
| A5 | 148 × 210 | 5 7/8 × 8 1/4 |
| A6 | 105 × 148 | 4 1/8 × 5 7/8 |
| A7 | 74 × 105 | 2 7/8 × 4 1/8 |
| A8 | 52 × 74 | 2 × 2 7/8 |

In addition to the preceding A sizes, there are two series from which A sizes can be cut. The series prefixed R and SR are designated as parent sheets for A sizes with tolerances for accommodating bleeds and extra trims.

### ISO R AND SR SHEET SIZES AND INCH EQUIVALENTS

| ISO Size | Size (millimeters) | Size (inches) *approx.* |
|---|---|---|
| RA0 | 860 × 1220 | 33 $7/8$ × 48 $1/8$ |
| RA1 | 610 × 860 | 24 $1/8$ × 33 $7/8$ |
| RA2 | 430 × 610 | 17 × 24 |
| SRA0 | 900 × 128 | 35 $1/2$ × 50 $3/8$ |
| SRA1 | 640 × 900 | 25 $1/4$ × 35 $1/2$ |
| SRA2 | 450 × 640 | 17 $7/8$ × 25 $1/4$ |

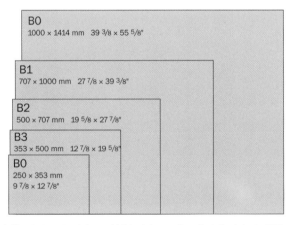

The B series is about half way between two A sizes and is intended as an alternative to the A sheets. ISO B series sheets are narrower than the A series and are usually used for posters and wall charts. The B series is based on a B0 size of 1000 × 1414 mm.

### ISO B SHEET SIZES AND INCH EQUIVALENTS

| ISO Size | Size (millimeters) | Size (inches) approx. |
|---|---|---|
| B0 | 1000 × 1414 | 39 $3/8$ × 55 $5/8$ |
| B1 | 707 × 1000 | 27 $7/8$ × 39 $3/8$ |
| B2 | 500 × 707 | 19 $5/8$ × 27 $7/8$ |
| B3 | 353 × 500 | 12 $7/8$ × 19 $5/8$ |
| B4 | 250 × 353 | 9 $7/8$ × 12 $7/8$ |
| B5 | 176 × 250 | 7 × 9 $7/8$ |
| B6 | 125 × 176 | 5 × 7 |
| B7 | 88 × 125 | 3 $1/2$ × 5 |
| B8 | 62 × 88 | 2 $1/2$ × 3 $1/2$ |

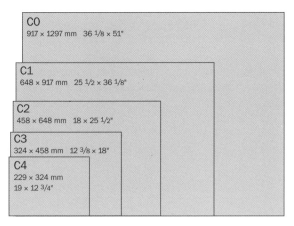

**C0**
917 × 1297 mm   36 1/8 × 51"

**C1**
648 × 917 mm   25 1/2 × 36 1/8"

**C2**
458 × 648 mm   18 × 25 1/2"

**C3**
324 × 458 mm   12 3/8 × 18"

**C4**
229 × 324 mm
19 × 12 3/4"

The C series is used for folders, postcards, and envelopes suitable for stationery in the A sizes. (For more information on the C series as it pertains to envelopes, see Chapter 8, Envelopes and Folders.)

## ISO C SHEET SIZES AND INCH EQUIVALENTS

| ISO Size | Size (millimeters) | Size (inches) *approx.* |
|----------|--------------------|-------------------------|
| C0 | 917 × 1297 | 36 1/8 × 51 |
| C1 | 648 × 917 | 25 1/2 × 36 1/8 |
| C2 | 458 × 648 | 18 × 25 |
| C3 | 324 × 458 | 12 3/4 × 18 |
| C4 | 229 × 324 | 9 × 12 1/2 |
| C5 | 162 × 229 | 6 3/8 × 9 |
| C6 | 114 × 162 | 4 1/2 × 6 3/8 |
| C7 | 81 × 114 | 3 1/4 × 4 1/2 |
| C8 | 57 × 81 | 2 1/4 × 3 1/4 |

## BASIS WEIGHT EQUIVALENTS

In North America, the term *basis weight* or *ream weight* is used to define the weight in pounds of a ream of paper cut to a given size. (A ream is defined as five hundred sheets of the basic size of a paper.) Basis weight is stated in pounds as represented by the # symbol.

The basic size of a sheet varies according to its grade. (Note that the basic size is only one of many standard sizes for each grade and is only used as a means of determining basis weight.) Basic sizes used to determine basis weight of some common papers are listed below:

| Paper type | Sheet size |
| --- | --- |
| Bond, ledger, and writing | 17 × 22 inches |
| Uncoated book and text | 25 × 38 inches |
| Coated book | 25 × 38 inches |
| Cover | 20 × 26 inches |
| Bristol | 22 1/2 × 28 1/2 inches |
| Kraft, tag, and newsprint | 24 × 36 inches |

Because of the size variations, paper grades that share the same basis weight may not look and feel as though they share the same basis weight. For instance, when comparing a sheet of 65# text and 65# cover stock, the cover stock will look and feel much heavier.

The following list of equivalents should help to define the basis weight differences between various grades.

| Paper grade | Equivalent to |
| --- | --- |
| 16# bond | 40# text |
| 20# bond | 50# text |
| 24# bond | 60# text |
| 28# bond | 70# text |
| | |
| 90# text | 50# cover |
| 100# text | 55# cover |
| 110# text | 60# cover |
| 120# text | 65# cover |

## GRAMMAGE

Outside of North America, the weight of paper is measured in grams per square meter (gsm). The grammage system measures the weights of all papers without taking into consideration their size or grade. This system standardizes a ream at five hundred sheets and defines a sheet as 1 square meter (A size). The term grammage is used to define the basis weight of all grades of paper measured in grams per square meter.

The following list gives some basis weight and grammage equivalents. Because North American basis weights are based on different basic sizes, the progression of weight conversion may not seem to be as logical as the basis weight comparisons on the opposite page.

| Paper grade | Equivalent to | Paper grade | Equivalent to |
|---|---|---|---|
| 16# bond | 59 gsm | 60# cover | 162 gsm |
| 24# bond | 89 gsm | 65# cover | 176 gsm |
| | | 80# cover | 216 gsm |
| 67# bristol | 148 gsm | 100# cover | 270 gsm |
| 80# bristol | 178 gsm | 120# cover | 325 gsm |
| 100# bristol | 219 gsm | | |
| 120# bristol | 263 gsm | 90# index | 163 gsm |
| 140# bristol | 307 gsm | 110# index | 199 gsm |
| | | 140# index | 253 gsm |
| 30# text | 44 gsm | 170# index | 308 gsm |
| 40# text | 59 gsm | | |
| 45# text | 67 gsm | | |
| 60# text | 89 gsm | | |
| 70# text | 104 gsm | | |
| 80# text | 118 gsm | | |
| 100# text | 148 gsm | | |

### Converting Basis Weight to Grammage

To convert the basis weight of a paper to its grammage, look up the sheet size in the left-hand column of the chart below. "Lb." means pounds (basis weight).

| Size (inches) | Basis weight to grammage | Grammage to basis weight |
|---|---|---|
| 17 × 22 | 3.760 × lb. = gsm | 0.266 × gsm = lb. |
| 20 × 26 | 2.704 × lb. = gsm | 0.370 × gsm = lb. |
| 22 × 28 | 2.282 × lb. = gsm | 0.438 × gsm = lb. |
| 22 1/2 × 28 1/2 | 2.195 × lb. = gsm | 0.456 × gsm = lb. |
| 24 × 36 | 1.627 × lb. = gsm | 0.614 × gsm = lb. |
| 25 × 38 | 1.48 × lb. = gsm | 0.675 × gsm = lb. |

## CALIPER, BULK, AND PPI

Paper thickness is defined as caliper. Caliper is measured in thousandths of an inch and expressed as point size. One point equals 0.001 inch. Stock that is 0.007 inches thick is described as 7 point or 7 pt. Points are most often used when referring to cover stock. It is also used by the US Postal Service, which states its thickness requirements in calipers.

The term *bulk* is used to refer to the thickness of paper relative to its paper weight. A paper's finish will have an impact on its bulk. For instance, coated papers tend to be thinner than uncoated papers and have less bulk for their basis weight.

Publishers often state bulk as pages per inch, or ppi. Below is a comparison chart that compares caliper size with pages per inch.

| Caliper | Pages per inch (ppi) |
| --- | --- |
| 0.0020 | 1000 |
| 0.0024 | 842 |
| 0.0028 | 726 |
| 0.0034 | 592 |
| 0.0038 | 532 |
| 0.0042 | 470 |
| 0.0046 | 432 |
| 0.0050 | 400 |
| 0.0054 | 372 |
| 0.0060 | 332 |

## Basis Weight/Caliper Equivalents

The following chart gives an approximate caliper thickness for the different basis weights of some common papers. Because a paper's finish also affects its thickness or bulk, calipers are also given for common finishes.

| Basis Weight | Coated | Smooth | Vellum | Textured |
|---|---|---|---|---|
| Bond/Writing | | | | |
| 13# | | 0.0021 | 0.0025 | 0.0027 |
| 16# | | 0.0026 | 0.0031 | 0.0033 |
| 20# | | 0.0032 | 0.0039 | 0.0042 |
| 24# | | 0.0038 | 0.0047 | 0.0050 |
| | | | | |
| Index | | | | |
| 90# | | 0.0080 | 0.0084 | |
| 110# | | 0.0096 | 0.0104 | |
| 140# | | 0.0132 | 0.0140 | |
| 170# | | 0.0144 | 0.0160 | |
| | | | | |
| Book/Text | | | | |
| 40# | | 0.0025 | 0.0031 | 0.0034 |
| 50# | 0.0023 | 0.0031 | 0.0038 | 0.0041 |
| 60# | 0.0028 | 0.0038 | 0.0046 | 0.0050 |
| 70# | 0.0034 | 0.0044 | 0.0054 | 0.0058 |
| 80# | 0.0040 | 0.0050 | 0.0059 | 0.0065 |
| 90# | 0.0046 | 0.0057 | 0.0065 | 0.0074 |
| 100# | 0.0052 | 0.0063 | 0.0071 | 0.0082 |
| 120# | 0.0060 | 0.0076 | 0.0082 | 0.0100 |
| | | | | |
| Cover | | | | |
| 50# | | 0.0058 | 0.0070 | 0.0075 |
| 80# | 0.0072 | 0.0093 | 0.0113 | 0.0120 |
| 100# | 0.0092 | 0.0116 | 0.0140 | 0.0150 |

PPI FORMULA

Determining pages per inch can be important for determining the thickness of a finished publication. To calculate the number of pages per inch, calculate the caliper (points) of eight pages (four sheets) than divide the number of points into eight. In the following example, four sheets of a hypothetical paper measures 0.016 inches in thickness.

*Example:* 8.000 ÷ 0.016 = 500 ppi

## FINISHES

In addition to considering basis weight or grammage, caliper, and sheet size, paper comes in finishes that range from smooth to textured. Uncoated papers also come in an assortment of finishes that are embossed into the paper as it is dried. These include linen, laid, and cockle textures.

Coated papers are available in uncalendered (an unpolished coated surface), machine calendered (a smoother finish), and supercalendared (highly polished) finishes—processes that affect the smoothness or glossiness of the surface. These can range from a matte or dull-coat finish to the high-gloss sheen of a cast-coated stock.

## GRAIN

Grain refers to the alignment of the fibers on a given sheet of paper. The grain direction of a paper can affect folding accuracy and degree of stiffness. Paper tears and folds more easily when it is torn or folded with the direction of the grain. Folding paper against the grain can result in a rough or uneven fold. Business cards cut so that the length of the card runs in the direction of the grain tend to feel flimsier than cards cut with their length against the grain. It's best to check with your printer to determine the best way to set up your document for optimum grain direction.

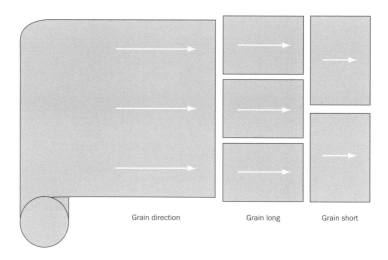

Grain direction       Grain long       Grain short

Paper is manufactured on rolls with the fibers aligned parallel to the edge of the roll. Sheets are cut from these rolls. When fibers are parallel to the length of the sheet, the stock is described as grain long. When fibers run parallel to the width of a sheet, the stock is grain short. Grain direction can affect printing stability, and long-grain sheets are generally preferred for multicolored jobs. Printing press sizes can sometimes necessitate the use of short-grained paper, so it's best to check with your printer before preparing your files.

## GETTING THE MOST FROM A SHEET

Minimizing wasted trim involves understanding how many trimmed pages will fit on a standard paper size. Use the following chart to determine how many pages will fit on North American standard paper sizes. (Note: Trim size does not include bleed allowances.)

| Trimmed Page Size of Finished Piece Inches (and millimeters) | Number of Pages in Finished Piece | Number of Finished Pieces from Each Sheet | Paper Size Inches (and millimeters) |
|---|---|---|---|
| 9 × 12 (228.6 × 304.8 mm) | 16 | 2 | 38 × 50 (965 × 1269 mm) |
| | 8 | 2 | 25 × 38 (635 × 965 mm) |
| | 4 | 4 | 25 × 38 (635 × 965 mm) |
| 8 1/2 × 11 (215.9 × 279.4 mm) | 16 | 2 | 35 × 45 (888 × 1142 mm) |
| | 8 | 2 | 23 × 35 (584 × 888 mm) |
| | 4 | 4 | 23 × 35 (584 × 888 mm) |
| 8 × 10 (203.2 × 254 mm) | 4 | 8 | 35 × 45 (888 × 1142 mm) |
| | 8 | 4 | 35 × 45 (888 × 1142 mm) |
| | 16 | 2 | 35 × 45 (888 × 1142 mm) |
| 6 × 9 (152.4 × 228.6 mm) | 32 | 2 | 38 × 50 (965 × 1269 mm) |
| | 16 | 2 | 25 × 38 (635 × 965 mm) |
| | 8 | 4 | 25 × 38 (635 × 965 mm) |
| | 4 | 8 | 25 × 38 (635 × 965 mm) |
| 6 × 4 1/2 (152.4 × 114.3 mm) | 32 | 2 | 25 × 38 (635 × 965 mm) |
| | 16 | 4 | 25 × 38 (635 × 965 mm) |
| | 8 | 8 | 25 × 38 (635 × 965 mm) |
| | 4 | 16 | 25 × 38 (635 × 965 mm) |
| 5 × 8 (127 × 203.2 mm) | 4 | 16 | 35 × 45 (888 × 1142 mm) |
| | 8 | 8 | 35 × 45 (888 × 1142 mm) |
| | 32 | 2 | 35 × 45 (888 × 1142 mm) |
| 4 1/4 × 5 3/8 (107.95 × 136.53 mm) | 32 | 4 | 35 × 45 (888 × 1142 mm) |
| | 16 | 8 | 35 × 45 (888 × 1142 mm) |
| | 8 | 16 | 35 × 45 (888 × 1142 mm) |
| | 4 | 32 | 35 × 45 (888 × 1142 mm) |
| 4 × 9 (101.6 × 228.6 mm) | 24 | 2 | 25 × 38 (635 × 965 mm) |
| | 16 | 6 | 38 × 50 (965 × 1269 mm) |
| | 12 | 4 | 25 × 38 (635 × 965 mm) |
| | 8 | 12 | 38 × 50 (965 × 1269 mm) |
| | 4 | 12 | 25 × 38 (635 × 965 mm) |

## PAPER ESTIMATOR

Consult the chart for determining how many pieces can be cut from a single sheet of paper (see page 67), then refer to this chart for estimating the amount of paper needed for a given quantity. To determine how many sheets of paper will be needed for a job, check the number that will fit on a single sheet in the left-hand column. Then find the corresponding quantity by reading across on the top column (Example: If sixteen pieces will fit on a single sheet, printing a quantity of three thousand would require 188 sheets of paper.) Note that quantities given do not account for spoilage. Spoilage percentages are usually determined by individual printers, depending on the length and complexity of the pressrun and the complexity of the binding process.

| Number Out of Sheet | Quantity of Pressrun 500 | 1M | 1.5M | 2M | 2.5M | 3M | 3.5M | 4M | 4.5M | 5M |
|---|---|---|---|---|---|---|---|---|---|---|
| 2 | 250 | 500 | 750 | 1000 | 1250 | 1500 | 1750 | 2000 | 2250 | 2500 |
| 3 | 167 | 334 | 500 | 667 | 834 | 1000 | 1167 | 1334 | 1500 | 1667 |
| 4 | 125 | 250 | 375 | 500 | 625 | 750 | 875 | 1000 | 1125 | 1250 |
| 5 | 100 | 200 | 300 | 400 | 500 | 600 | 700 | 800 | 900 | 1000 |
| 6 | 84 | 167 | 250 | 334 | 417 | 599 | 584 | 667 | 750 | 834 |
| 7 | 72 | 143 | 215 | 286 | 358 | 429 | 500 | 572 | 643 | 715 |
| 8 | 63 | 125 | 188 | 250 | 313 | 375 | 438 | 500 | 563 | 625 |
| 9 | 56 | 112 | 167 | 223 | 278 | 334 | 389 | 445 | 500 | 556 |
| 10 | 50 | 100 | 150 | 200 | 250 | 300 | 350 | 400 | 450 | 500 |
| 11 | 46 | 91 | 137 | 182 | 228 | 273 | 319 | 364 | 410 | 455 |
| 12 | 42 | 84 | 126 | 168 | 209 | 250 | 292 | 334 | 375 | 417 |
| 13 | 39 | 77 | 116 | 154 | 193 | 231 | 270 | 308 | 347 | 385 |
| 14 | 36 | 72 | 108 | 144 | 179 | 215 | 250 | 286 | 322 | 358 |
| 15 | 34 | 67 | 100 | 134 | 167 | 200 | 234 | 267 | 300 | 334 |
| 16 | 32 | 63 | 94 | 125 | 157 | 188 | 219 | 250 | 282 | 313 |
| 17 | 30 | 59 | 89 | 118 | 148 | 177 | 206 | 236 | 265 | 295 |
| 18 | 28 | 56 | 84 | 112 | 139 | 167 | 195 | 223 | 250 | 279 |
| 19 | 27 | 53 | 79 | 106 | 132 | 156 | 185 | 211 | 237 | 264 |
| 20 | 25 | 50 | 75 | 100 | 125 | 150 | 175 | 200 | 225 | 250 |
| 21 | 24 | 48 | 72 | 96 | 120 | 143 | 167 | 191 | 216 | 239 |
| 22 | 23 | 46 | 69 | 91 | 114 | 137 | 160 | 182 | 205 | 228 |
| 23 | 22 | 44 | 66 | 87 | 109 | 131 | 153 | 174 | 196 | 218 |
| 24 | 21 | 42 | 63 | 84 | 105 | 126 | 146 | 167 | 186 | 209 |
| 25 | 20 | 40 | 60 | 80 | 100 | 120 | 140 | 160 | 180 | 200 |
| 26 | 20 | 39 | 58 | 77 | 97 | 116 | 135 | 154 | 174 | 193 |
| 27 | 19 | 38 | 56 | 75 | 93 | 112 | 130 | 149 | 167 | 186 |
| 28 | 18 | 36 | 54 | 72 | 90 | 108 | 125 | 143 | 161 | 179 |
| 29 | 18 | 36 | 54 | 72 | 87 | 103 | 121 | 138 | 156 | 173 |
| 30 | 17 | 34 | 51 | 67 | 84 | 100 | 117 | 134 | 150 | 167 |
| 31 | 17 | 33 | 49 | 65 | 81 | 97 | 113 | 139 | 146 | 162 |
| 32 | 16 | 32 | 47 | 63 | 79 | 94 | 110 | 126 | 141 | 167 |

## PAPER USAGE GUIDE

Use the following chart as a general reference guide for determining which papers are most suitable for a given job.

| Paper Type/ Standard Size | Characteristics/ Colors | Finishes | Typical Sizes (in inches) | Basis Weights | Primary Uses |
|---|---|---|---|---|---|
| Bond 17 × 22 (43.2 × 55.9 cm) | Comes in a range of pastels, neutrals, matching envelopes, and cover weights | Smooth, cockle | 8 1/2 × 11, 8 1/2 × 14, 11 × 17, 17 × 22, 17 × 28, 19 × 24, 19 × 28, 23 × 35 rolls | 16, 20, 24 | Fliers, forms, photocopies, newsletters |
| Writing paper 17 × 22 (43.2 × 55.9 cm) | Comes in a range of colors and flocking options that match envelopes, plus cover and text weights | Smooth, linen laid, vellum, cockle, and more | 8 1/2 × 11, 17 × 22, 22 1/2 × 35, 23 × 35, 25 × 38 | 24, 28 | Stationery |
| Uncoated book 25 × 38 (63.5 × 96.5 cm) | Comes in a range of colors and is thicker and more opaque than bond or writing papers | Smooth | 8 1/2 × 11, 8 1/2 × 14, 17 1/2 × 22 1/2, 23 × 29, 22 1/2 × 35, 23 × 35, 25 × 38, 35 × 45, 38 × 50 rolls | 30, 32, 35, 40, 45, 50, 60, 65, 70, 80 | Books, direct mail, newsletters, catalogs |
| Text 25 × 38 (63.5 × 96.5 cm) | Comes in a range of colors and flocking options that match envelopes, plus cover and text weights | Smooth, linen laid, vellum, cockle, and more | 8 1/2 × 11, 17 1/2 × 22 1/2, 23 × 35, 25 × 38, 26 × 40 | 60, 65, 70, 75, 80, 100 | Letterhead, annual reports, invitations, posters, brochures, direct mail, books |
| Coated book 25 × 38 (63.5 × 96.5 cm) | Matching cover weights limited to white and cream although specialty lines exist in a range of colors | Dull, gloss, matte, cast-coated, some embossed finishes | 19 × 25, 23 × 29, 23 × 35, 25 × 38, 35 × 45, 38 × 50 | 40, 45, 50, 60, 70, 80, 100 | Magazines, catalogs, books, direct mail, annual reports |
| Cover 20 × 26 (50.8 × 66 cm) | Heavier and more durable counterpart to coordinate with text, book, and writing papers | Smooth, cockle, linen laid, vellum, dull, gloss, matte, cast-coated | 20 × 26, 23 × 35, 35 × 38, 26 × 40 | 60, 65, 80, 100, 120, 130 | Business cards, covers for annual reports, brochures, menus, tickets, postcards, pocket folders, greeting cards |
| Index/Bristol 22 × 28 1/2 (57.2 × 72.4 cm) | Comes in a range of colors and finishes | Coated, vellum, smooth | 22 × 28, 22 1/2 × 28 1/2, 23 × 35, 24 × 36, 25 1/2 × 30 1/2, 28 × 44 | 67, 90, 100, 110, 125, 140, 150, 175 | Postcards, file folders, index cards, boxes, tickets, clothing tags |
| Translucent vellum | Semitransparent stock comes in a range of colors and weights plus matching envelopes | Smooth, grooved | 8 1/2 × 11, 23 × 35, 25 × 38 | 17, 21 1/4, 24, 27, 29, 40, 48, 53 | Fly sheets, overlays, see-thru envelopes for invitations and other mailings |
| Newsprint 24 × 36 (61 × 91.5 cm) | Inexpensive, lightweight, white/manila only | Vellum | Rolls | 30 | Newspapers, tabloids |
| Label | Comes in gummed, pressure sensitive, and self-adhesive backing and in a range of colors | Smooth (uncoated), matte, dull, glossy, and cast-coated | 8 1/2 × 11, 17 × 22, 20 × 26, 24 × 30 rolls | 60, 70 | Labels, signs, stickers |
| Kraft 24 × 36 (61 × 91.5 cm) | Strong and durable, brown/manila only | Vellum | Rolls | 30, 40, 50 | Bags, envelopes |

# ○ Chapter 7: Bindings, Bleeds, and Folds

## STANDARD BINDING TYPES

There are many ways to bind loose sheets, folded sheets, or signatures together—each with its own set of aesthetic, cost, and durability considerations. Here is an overview of the binding options most readily available. Consult the chart following this section to compare the cost, durability, and aesthetic attributes of these binding methods.

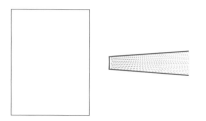

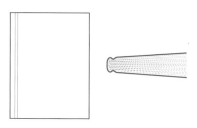

PERFECT BINDING

Signatures are gathered in a stack rather than nested. The spine side of the stack is milled to remove the folded edges. Melted adhesive is applied along the spine edges of the pages. The cover is applied while the glue is hot and wrapped around the book. The book is trimmed on a three-knife trimmer.

CASE BINDING (SMYTHE SEWN)

Gathered signatures are assembled and sewn along the spine. The sewn book block is then glued on the spine and trimmed on three sides. The trimmed book block is then glued to an outer cover or case, which is manufactured separately. The case is held to the book block by end-sheets attached to the first and last signatures and glued to the inside covers.

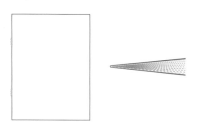

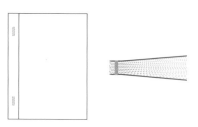

SADDLE STITCH BINDING

Cover and signatures are nested one within the other and hung over a chain or "saddle." Covers are scored and folded on the same machine and then laid on top of the signatures. Cover and signatures are wire stitched (stapled) at the center of the spine, and then trimmed.

SIDE STITCH BINDING

Cover and individual pages or signatures are collated and assembled into a stack and then wire stitched (stapled) at the bound edge.

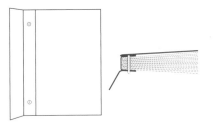

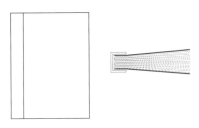

**SCREW AND POST BINDING**
Cover and signatures or individual pages are collated and assembled in a stack and trimmed on all sides, then drilled and fastened together with posts held on by screws. Screws can be unscrewed to add or remove pages as needed.

**TAPE BINDING**
Signatures and covers are assembled, collated, and trimmed on all sides. A strip of flexible cloth tape that contains glue is applied on the edges of the spine and heated. The glue melts and spreads, gluing the covers and signatures together.

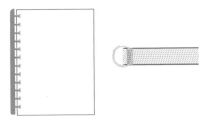

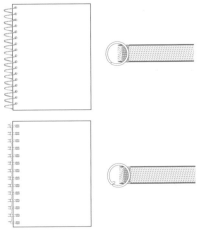

**PLASTIC COMB BINDING**
Trimmed covers and individual pages are assembled, collated, and held together by a plastic comb that is opened, inserted into drilled holes, and then closed. Comb can be opened to insert more pages as needed.

**SPIRAL AND DOUBLE-LOOP WIRE BINDING**
Trimmed covers and individual pages are assembled, collated, and held together by a spiraled piece of plastic, wire, or doubled wire inserted into drilled holes.

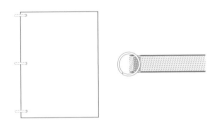

**RING BINDING**
Trimmed covers and individual pages are assembled, collated, and held together by individual rings. Or individual pages are assembled, collated, and inserted into a binder with rings. Rings and binders come in a variety of sizes and colors. Pages can be added or subtracted as needed.

## Which Binding Method Works Best?

Bindings differ in their appearance, cost, and function. Some binding styles are suitable for publications with many pages, whereas, others will only work for those with a limited number of pages. Some methods allow pages to lie flat, whereas, others don't. Durability and cost are other considerations. Saddle stitching, for instance, is relatively inexpensive but not as permanent as case binding. The following chart should give you a better idea of which options will best suit your publication's design and budget.

| Binding Style | Girth | Lays Flat | Printable Spine | Durability | Relative Cost | Advantages | Limitations |
|---|---|---|---|---|---|---|---|
| CASE | 3" for hardcover, $1\frac{3}{4}$" for paperback | Yes | Yes | High | High | Strength, durability, and a look of quality. | Most costly option. Requires more production time. Requires signatures. |
| PERFECT | Up to $2\frac{3}{8}$" | No | Yes, for $\frac{1}{8}$" and larger | Moderate | Low | Inexpensive for moderate runs of of 1,000–5,000. Can bind single sheets. | Paper grain must run parallel to the binding edge. Image area may be lost in gutter. |
| SADDLE STITCH | Up to $\frac{1}{2}$" | Yes | No | Moderate | Low | Fast and inexpensive. Can easily accommodate inserts. | Requires signatures. Pages must be in increments of four. May need adjustments for creep. |
| SIDE STITCH | Up to 1" | No | No | High | Low | Fast and inexpensive. Variety of wire styles and widths available. | Pages won't lie flat when open. Requires a minimum 1" margin. |
| SCREW AND POST | Up to 1" | No | No | High | High | Easy to insert additional pages. Can accommodate pages of different materials. | Hand-assembly is time consuming and not appropriate for large quantities. |
| TAPE | Up to $1\frac{3}{4}$" | Yes | No | Moderate | High | Durable option that is less costly than case binding. Tape comes in a range of colors. | Requires signatures. Pages must be in increments of four. |
| PLASTIC COMB | Up to $1\frac{3}{4}$" | Yes | Possible with foil stamping | Low | Low for small runs | Widely available. Can be reopened to insert other pages. Facing pages align. | Time-consuming and costly for large quantities. |
| SPIRAL | Up to 2" and folds over 360˚ | Yes | No | Moderate | Moderate | Well suited to short runs. Can accommodate pages of different materials. | Because of jogging, crossover designs may not align. |
| RING | Up to 3" | Yes | Binders can be screen printed | Low | Cost of materials for in-house hand assembly | Easy to insert additional pages. Can accommodate pages of different materials. | Hand assembly is inappropriate for large runs, but good for custom applications. |

## Common Fold Styles

Fold styles have standard names that should be used when communicating with printers and binderies. Following is a list of some of the most common styles and their names.

FOUR-PAGE SIMPLE FOLD

One fold made along either the short or long dimension of the paper resulting in four panels or pages.

FOUR-PAGE SHORT FOLD

A simple fold made asymmetrically so that two pages or panels are larger than the others.

SIX-PAGE ACCORDION FOLD

Two simple folds where one fold bends in the opposite direction of the other resulting in six panels or pages. Accordion folds can comprise six, eight, ten, and sometimes twelve panels or pages.

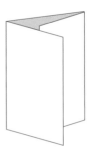

SIX-PAGE BARREL OR ROLL FOLD

Two simple folds where the outer edges of each panel or page are folded in toward the other resulting in six panels or pages. Barrel or roll folds composed of more than six panels or pages are often called rolling folds and can consist of many panels or pages.

## PAPER GRAIN CAN AFFECT FOLDING

*Heavy text and cover stock needs to be scored before it's folded, preferably in the direction of the grain. Folding against the grain, even with a score, may result in problems. To determine the grain direction of your sheet, fold it vertically and then horizontally. When it's folded with the grain, the fold line will be much more even than when it's folded against the grain.*

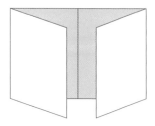

EIGHT-PAGE GATEFOLD

A barrel fold with an additional fold in the center, resulting in eight panels or pages.

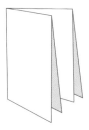

EIGHT-PAGE FRENCH FOLD/SIXTEEN-PAGE SIGNATURE

Multiple fold where the paper is first folded in one direction, then folded perpendicular to the first fold. This configuration is also used when creating sixteen-page signatures.

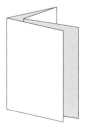

EIGHT-PAGE PARALLEL FOLD

A combination of a barrel fold and an accordion fold that forms eight panels or pages.

## Tolerances for Gatefolds, Barrel, or Roll Folds

Gatefolds, as well as barrel or roll folds, require special allowances so that the outer panels or pages of a piece will overlap those within. Although the following standards apply to text weight papers, tolerances may vary slightly with other types of paper.

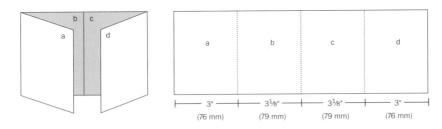

Gatefolds require an additional 1/8 inch (3.175 mm) on the outer panels (b and c) in the fold sequence.

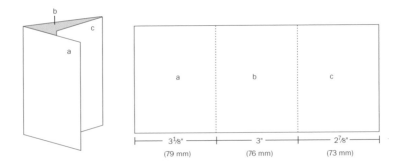

Roll or barrel folds require an additional 1/8 inch (3.175 mm) for each panel in the fold sequence so that each panel is 1/8 inch (3.175 mm) larger than the next.

## ENVELOPE CONSTRUCTION

This diagram shows the basic parts of an envelope. Refer to these terms when working with envelope converters or others involved in envelope printing and manufacturing.

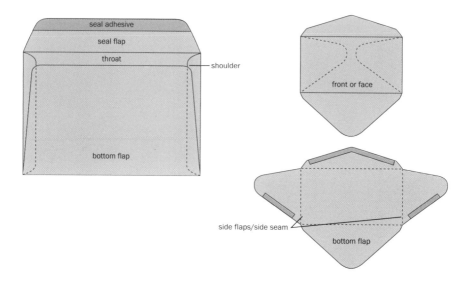

## CLOSURE DESIGNATION

Closure designation is described by the location of the envelope opening and seal flap. Aesthetic and functional considerations should guide your decision on which of the following types to select.

OPEN END (OE)

The opening and seal flap are located on the short dimension. Open-end envelopes are well suited to hand-insertion applications.

OPEN SIDE (OS)

The opening and seal flap are located on the long dimension. Open-side envelopes are well suited to automatic as well as hand-insertion applications.

## Standard Envelope Styles and Sizes

Envelopes come in a variety of styles that vary according to function. Some styles are more suitable for invitations and announcements, while others are appropriate for business use. Each style is available in a range of standard sizes. Consult the diagrams and listings below to determine which style and type of envelope is best for your job.

COMMERCIAL AND OFFICIAL (UNITED STATES)

Standard correspondence-style envelopes. Open-sided with gummed flaps. Made in a wide range of bond and kraft. Commercial sizes range from No. 5 to No. 6 3/4. Official sizes range from No. 7 to No. 14.

BOOKLET (UNITED STATES)

For use with booklets, folders, and other types of direct mail. Open-side design permits overall printing.

| Item/No. | Size (inches) | Size (centimeters) |
|---|---|---|
| 5 | 3 $^1/_{16}$ × 5 $^1/_2$ | 7.78 × 13.97 |
| 6 | 3 $^3/_8$ × 6 | 8.5725 × 15.24 |
| 6 $^1/_4$ | 3 $^1/_2$ × 6 | 8.89 × 15.24 |
| 6 $^1/_2$ | 3 $^9/_{16}$ × 6 $^1/_2$ | 9.05 × 16.51 |
| 6 $^3/_4$ | 3 $^5/_8$ × 6 $^1/_2$ | 9.2075 × 16.51 |
| 7 | 3 $^3/_4$ × 6 $^3/_4$ | 9.525 × 16.145 |
| 7 $^1/_2$ | 3 $^3/_4$ × 7 $^5/_8$ | 9.525 × 19.3675 |
| 7 $^3/_4$ (Monarch) | 3 $^7/_8$ × 7 $^1/_2$ | 9.8425 × 19.05 |
| Data Card | 3 $^1/_2$ × 7 $^5/_8$ | 8.89 × 19.3675 |
| 8 $^5/_8$ (Check) | 3 $^5/_8$ × 8 $^5/_8$ | 9.2075 × 21.9075 |
| 9 | 3 $^7/_8$ × 8 $^7/_8$ | 9.8425 × 22.5425 |
| 10 | 4 $^1/_8$ × 9 $^1/_2$ | 10.4775 × 24.13 |
| 10 $^1/_2$ | 4 $^1/_2$ × 9 $^1/_2$ | 11.43 × 24.13 |
| 11 | 4 $^1/_2$ × 10 $^3/_8$ | 11.43 × 26.3525 |
| 12 | 4 $^3/_4$ × 11 | 12.065 × 27.94 |
| 14 | 5 × 11 $^1/_2$ | 12.7 × 29.21 |

| Item/No. | Size (inches) | Size (centimeters) |
|---|---|---|
| 2 $^1/_2$ | 4 $^1/_2$ × 5 $^7/_8$ | 11.43 × 14.9225 |
| 3 | 4 $^3/_4$ × 6 $^1/_2$ | 12.065 × 16.51 |
| 4 $^1/_4$ | 5 × 7$^1/_2$ | 12.7 × 19.05 |
| 5 | 5 $^1/_2$ × 8 $^1/_2$ | 13.97 × 21.59 |
| 6 | 5 $^3/_4$ × 8 $^7/_8$ | 14.605 × 22.5425 |
| 6 $^1/_2$ | 6 × 9 | 15.24 × 22.86 |
| 6 $^3/_4$ | 6 $^1/_2$ × 9 $^1/_2$ | 16.51 × 24.13 |
| 7 | 6 $^1/_4$ × 9 $^5/_8$ | 15.875 × 24.44475 |
| 7 $^1/_4$ | 7 × 10 | 17.78 × 25.4 |
| 7 $^1/_2$ | 7 $^1/_2$ × 10 $^1/_2$ | 19.05 × 26.67 |
| 8 | 8 × 11 $^1/_8$ | 20.32 × 28.2575 |
| 9 | 8 $^3/_4$ × 11 $^1/_2$ | 22.225 × 29.21 |
| 9 $^1/_2$ | 9 × 12 | 22.86 × 30.48 |
| 10 | 9 $^1/_2$ × 12 $^5/_8$ | 24.13 × 32.0675 |
| 13 | 10 × 13 | 25.4 × 33.02 |

TICKET (UNITED STATES)

Open-side envelope for theater tickets. Often printed with advertising.

| Item/No. | Size (inches) | Size (centimeters) |
|---|---|---|
| 3 | 1 5/16 × 4 7/16 | 3.3350 × 11.2725 |

WINDOW (UNITED STATES)

Permit name and address typed on the enclosure to show through the window. Used for invoices, statements, checks, receipts, etc.

WINDOW (UNITED STATES)

| Item/No. | Size (inches) | Size (centimeters) |
|---|---|---|
| 6 1/4 | 3 1/2 × 6 | 8.89 × 15.24 |
| 6 3/4 | 3 5/8 × 6 1/2 | 9.2075 × 16.51 |
| 7 | 3 3/4 × 6 3/4 | 9.525 × 16.145 |
| 7 3/4 | 3 7/8 × 7 1/2 | 9.8425 × 19.05 |
| 8 5/8 | 3 5/8 × 8 7/8 | 9.2075 × 21.9075 |
| 9 | 3 7/8 × 8 7/8 | 9.8425 × 22.5425 |
| 10 | 4 1/8 × 9 1/2 | 10.4775 × 24.13 |
| 11 | 4 1/2 × 10 3/8 | 11.43 × 26.3525 |
| 12 | 4 3/4 × 11 | 12.065 × 27.94 |
| 14 | 5 × 11 1/2 | 12.7 × 29.21 |

**Window Size and Position (United States)**
Window size 4 3/4 × 1 1/8 inches (120.65 × 28.5 mm). Position 7/8 inches (22.2 mm) from left, 5/8 inches (15.87 mm) from bottom. Size 8 5/8 inches (219.0 mm) is 5/8 inches (15.87 mm) from left, 13/16 inches (20.6mm) from bottom.

WINDOW (CANADA)

| Item/No. | Size (inches) | Size (millimeters) |
|---|---|---|
| 8 | 3 5/8 × 6 1/2 | 92.075 × 165.1 |
| Banker's Check | 3 5/8 × 7 7/8 | 92.075 × 200.025 |
| Check | 3 5/8 × 8 5/8 | 92.075 × 219.075 |
| No. 8 1/2 | 3 3/4 × 6 3/4 | 95.25 × 161.45 |
| Large Check | 3 3/4 × 8 3/4 | 95.25 × 222.25 |
| Tu Fold | 4 × 7 1/2 | 101.6 × 190.5 |
| No. 9 | 4 × 9 | 101.6 × 228.6 |
| T-4 | 4 1/8 × 9 | 104.775 × 228.6 |
| No. 10 | 4 1/8 × 9 1/2 | 104.775 × 241.3 |
| Broker Window | 4 1/8 × 9 1/2 | 104.775 × 241.3 |
| No. 11 | 4 1/2 × 9 5/8 | 114.3 × 244.475 |

REMITTANCE (UNITED STATES)

CATALOG (UNITED STATES)

Large flap can be printed to contain any message. Used for coupons, credit information, applications, statements, etc.

| Item/No. | Size (inches) | Size (centimeters) |
|---|---|---|
| 6 1/4 | 3 1/2 × 6 | 8.89 × 15.24 |
| | (3 3/8 flap) | (7.9375 flap) |
| 6 1/2 | 3 1/2 × 6 1/4 | 8.89 × 15.5575 |
| | (3 3/8 flap) | (8.5725 flap) |
| 6 3/4 | 3 5/8 × 6 1/2 | 9.2075 × 16.51 |
| | (3 1/2 flap) | (8.89 flap) |
| 9 | 3 7/8 × 8 7/8 | 9.8425 × 22.5425 |

POLICY (UNITED STATES)

Primarily used for insurance policies. Also used to hold bonds, mortgages, and other legal papers.

| Item/No. | Size (inches) | Size (millimeters) |
|---|---|---|
| 9 | 4 × 9 | 101.6 × 228.6 |
| 10 | 4 1/8 × 9 1/2 | 104.775 × 241.3 |
| 11 | 4 1/2 × 10 3/8 | 114.3 × 263.25 |
| 12 | 4 3/4 × 10 7/8 | 276.225 × 276.2 |
| 14 | 5 × 11 1/2 | 127 × 292.1 |

Open-end style. Wide seams with heavy gummed flaps provide good protection for mail handling of catalogs, magazines, reports, etc.

| Item/No. | Size (inches) | Size (millimeters) |
|---|---|---|
| 1 | 6 × 9 | 152.4 × 228.6 |
| 1 3/4 | 6 1/2 × 9 1/2 | 165.1 × 241.3 |
| 2 | 6 1/2 × 10 | 165.1 × 254 |
| 3 | 7 × 10 | 177.8 × 254 |
| 6 | 7 1/2 × 10 1/2 | 190.5 × 266.7 |
| 7 | 8 × 11 | 203.2 × 279.4 |
| 8 | 8 1/4 × 11 1/4 | 209.55 × 285.75 |
| 9 1/2 | 8 1/2 × 10 1/2 | 215.9 × 266.7 |
| 9 3/4 | 8 3/4 × 11 1/4 | 222.25 × 285.75 |
| 10 1/2 | 9 × 12 | 228.6 × 304.8 |
| 12 1/2 | 9 1/2 × 12 1/2 | 241.3 × 317.5 |
| 13 1/2 | 10 × 13 | 254 × 330.2 |
| 14 1/4 | 11 1/4 × 14 1/4 | 285.75 × 361.95 |
| 14 1/2 | 11 1/2 × 14 1/2 | 292.1 × 368.3 |

METAL CLASP (UNITED STATES)

Strong and durable. Ideal for mailing bulky papers and heavy publications. Can be opened and closed many times.

| Item/No. | Size (inches) | Size (millimeters) |
|---|---|---|
| 0 | 2 $^1/_2$ × 4 × $^1/_4$ | 63.5 × 104.775 |
| 5 | 3 $^1/_8$ × 5 $^1/_2$ | 79.375 × 139.7 |
| 10 | 3 $^3/_8$ × 6 | 85.725 × 152.4 |
| 11 | 4 $^1/_2$ × 10 $^3/_8$ | 114.3 × 263.525 |
| 14 | 5 × 11 $^1/_2$ | 127 × 292.1 |
| 15 | 4 × 6 $^3/_8$ | 101.6 × 161.925 |
| 25 | 4 $^5/_8$ × 6 $^3/_4$ | 117.474 × 171.45 |
| 35 | 5 × 7 $^1/_2$ | 127 × 190.5 |
| 50 | 5 $^1/_2$ × 8 $^1/_4$ | 139.7 × 209.55 |
| 55 | 6 × 9 | 152.4 × 228.6 |
| 63 | 6 $^1/_2$ × 9 $^1/_2$ | 165.1 × 241.3 |
| 68 | 7 × 10 | 177.8 × 254 |
| 75 | 7 $^1/_2$ × 10 | 190.5 × 254 |
| 80 | 8 × 11 | 203.2 × 279.4 |
| 83 | 8 $^1/_2$ × 11 $^1/_2$ | 215.9 × 292.1 |
| 87 | 8 $^3/_4$ × 11 $^1/_4$ | 222.25 × 285.75 |
| 90 | 9 × 12 | 228.6 × 304.8 |
| 93 | 9 $^1/_2$ × 12 $^1/_2$ | 241.3 × 317.5 |
| 94 | 9 $^1/_4$ × 14 $^1/_2$ | 234.95 × 368.3 |
| 95 | 10 × 12 | 254 × 304.8 |
| 97 | 10 × 13 | 254 × 330.2 |
| 98 | 10 × 15 | 254 × 381 |
| 105 | 11 $^1/_2$ × 14 $^1/_2$ | 279.4 × 368.3 |
| 110 | 12 × 15 $^1/_2$ | 304.8 × 393.7 |

ANNOUNCEMENT OR A-STYLE

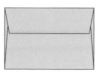

Made for use with a wide range of matching text and cover papers. May also have deckle (ragged cut) edge and flaps.

| Item/No. | Size (inches) | Size (millimeters) |
|---|---|---|
| A-2 | 4 $^3/_8$ × 5 $^3/_4$ | 111.125 ×146.05 |
| A-6 | 4 $^3/_4$ × 6 $^1/_2$ | 120.65 × 165.1 |
| A-7 | 5 $^1/_4$ × 7 $^1/_4$ | 133.35 ×184.15 |
| A-8 | 5 $^1/_2$ × 8 $^1/_8$ | 139.7 × 206.375 |
| A-10 | 6 × 9 $^1/_2$ | 152.4 × 241.3 |
| A-Long | 3 $^7/_8$ × 8 $^7/_8$ | 98.425 × 225.425 |

WALLET FLAP

Mostly used by banks or investment firms for mailing statements and other documents. Deep flap and extra-wide gummed area offer protection to the contents.

| Item/No. | Size (inches) | Size (millimeters) |
|---|---|---|
| 10 | 4 $^1/_8$ × 9 $^1/_2$ | 104.775 × 241.3 |
| 11 | 4 $^1/_2$ ×10 $^3/_8$ | 114.3 × 263.525 |
| 12 | 4 $^3/_4$ × 11 | 120.65 × 279.4 |
| 14 | 5 × 11 $^1/_2$ | 127 × 292.1 |
| 16 | 6 × 12 | 1524 × 304.8 |

BUSINESS ANNOUNCEMENT AND BARONIAL

Formal envelopes with deep, pointed flaps. Widely used for invitations, formal announcements, greeting, and social cards.

| Item/No. | Size (inches) | Size (millimeters) |
|---|---|---|
| Gladstone | 3 $9/16$ × 5 $9/16$ | 90.500 × 141.300 |
| 4 Baronial | 3 $5/8$ × 5 $1/8$ | 92.075 × 130.175 |
| 5 Baronial | 4 $1/8$ × 5 $1/8$ | 104.775 × 130.175 |
| 5 $1/4$ Baronial | 4 $1/4$ × 5 $1/4$ | 107.95 × 133.35 |
| 53 | 4 $1/8$ × 6 $1/4$ | 104.775 × 158.75 |
| 5 $1/2$ Baronial | 4 $3/8$ × 5 $5/8$ | 111.125 × 142.875 |
| 6 Baronial | 5 × 6 $1/4$ | 127 × 158.75 |
| 110 | 5 × 7 $1/4$ | 127 × 180.975 |
| Lee | 5 $1/4$ × 7 $1/4$ | 133.35 × 184.15 |
| 137 | 5 $1/2$ × 8 $1/2$ | 139.7 × 215.9 |

COIN

Used for paper currency as well as coins by banks and corporations.

| Item/No. | Size (inches) | Size (millimeters) |
|---|---|---|
| 00 | 1 $11/16$ × 2 $3/4$ | 42.875 × 69.85 |
| 1 | 2 $1/4$ × 3 $1/2$ | 57.15 × 88.9 |
| 3 | 2 $1/2$ × 4 $1/4$ | 63.5 × 107.95 |
| 4 | 3 × 4 $1/2$ | 76.2 × 114.3 |
| 5 | 2 $7/8$ × 5 $1/4$ | 73.025 × 133.35 |
| 5 $1/2$ | 3 $1/4$ × 5 $1/2$ | 88.9 × 139.7 |
| 6 | 3 $3/8$ × 6 | 85.725 × 152.4 |
| 7 | 3 $1/2$ × 6 $1/2$ | 88.9 × 165.1 |

## International Envelope Sizes

International, or ISO, envelope sizes are based on folding A4 (210 × 297 mm, letterhead sized) paper into an envelope. Other sizes and how they fit when folded into the various ISO envelope sizes are shown below.

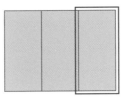

An A4 folded twice into thirds fits in a DL envelope.

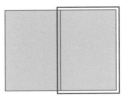

An A4 folded once fits in a C5 envelope.

An A5 folded once fits in a C6 envelope.

An A5 folded once fits in a DL envelope.

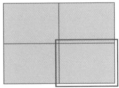

An A4 folded twice into quarters fits in a C6 envelope.

## PRINTING CONSIDERATIONS FOR ENVELOPES

• Paper mills and commercial printers rely on envelope converters to cut, fold, glue, and assemble envelopes. Envelopes are either premade by an envelope converter and sold by paper distributors as a product made from a mill's writing and text papers, or they are custom made by envelope converters from paper after it has been printed. Premade envelopes are less expensive than converting from flat sheets.

• Envelopes printed in four color, printed on the inside or covered entirely with exterior graphics need to be printed before they are converted into envelopes.

• Embossing or engraving will show through on the opposite side of a premade envelope, unless the tecnique is confined to the envelope flap. It is best to engrave or emboss before the envelope is converted.

• Printing, engraving, or embossing envelopes before conversion is more expensive and time consuming and not appropriate for small runs. However, if you plan to produce a quantity of 5,000 or more, printing before conversion may be within your budget. Anticipate at least three weeks for envelope conversion and check with your vendor to find out exactly what the time frame will be.

• When printing on premade envelopes, confine graphics and return address information to the upper-left corner of the envelope. Postal regulations require that the face of the envelope be left blank for address and postal information. A $^3/8$ inch (9.525 mm) allowance also needs to be made at the envelope's edges to accommodate press grippers.

Consult the following chart for standard ISO envelope sizes:

| Size | In millimeters | Approximate inches |
|------|----------------|--------------------|
| C3 | 324 × 458 | 12.76 × 18.03 |
| B4 | 250 × 353 | 9.84 × 13.89 |
| C4 | 229 × 324 | 9.01 × 12.76 |
| B5 | 176 × 250 | 6.93 × 9.84 |
| C5 | 162 × 229 | 6.38 × 9.01 |
| B6/C4 | 125 × 324 | 4.92 × 12.75 |
| B6 | 125 × 176 | 4.92 × 6.92 |
| C6 | 114 × 162 | 4.49 × 6.38 |
| DL | 110 × 220 | 4.33 × 8.66 |
| C7/C6 | 81 × 162 | 3.19 × 6.38 |
| C7 | 81 × 114 | 3.19 × 4.49 |

**Pocket Folder Styles**

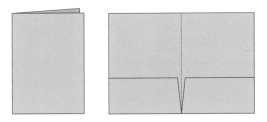

This two-pocket folder with glued flaps is an economical choice suitable for lightweight inserts, such as sample sheets or small brochures. It can be easily adapted to a one pocket configuration by eliminating one of the flaps. The business card slot can also be deleted if it isn't necessary. *For template see page 84*

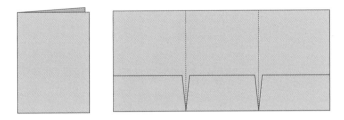

This three-pocket configuration folds to the same 9" x 12" (228.6 mm x 304.8 mm) size as the two-pocket configuration but opens to reveal an additional pocket. The folder features glued flaps at either end and an unglued flap on the center panel. *For template see page 85*

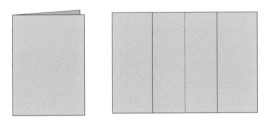

Square flaps can accommodate more inserts and bulkier documents than standard pocket folders. They work especially well for magazine media kits. Be sure to use heavy or laminated cover stock to achieve the necessary rigidity. *For template see page 86*

The following pocket folder templates are printed at $1/4$ scale. Enlarge them by 400% when scanning to bring them up to their actual size.

Template: Standard Two-Pocket Folder

Template: Two-Pocket Folder with Box Side Flaps

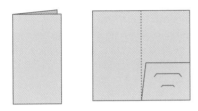

This single-pocket folder has slots to hold two types of room keys. It folds to fit in a jacket pocket or purse.

Template: Single-Pocket Room Key Folder

## PRINTING CONSIDERATIONS FOR POCKET FOLDERS

*Pocket folders offer a means of containing materials that will immediately add polish and professionalism to a presentation. However, they present some unique planning and production challenges.*

- *Pick a folder style and size that is suitable for your inserts. It's common to plan a folder with more or larger pockets than necessary with the assumption that too much space is better than not enough. However, pockets that are too large for their inserts will allow folder materials to move around, resulting in a messy presentation.*

- *For a sturdy folder, select a cover stock with a basis weight that is between 100 and 120 lb. (270 gsm, 325 gsm). Have a paper dummy made to determine if the stock you've chosen for your pocket folder will be suitable for the inserts.*

- *Box pocket folders and those with three panels often require hand assembly, a factor that will add time and expense to your job. Take this into consideration when determining the size and style of a folder.*

- *Most commercial printers have dies for pocket folders on hand, or use a vendor with a selection from which to choose. To save time and money, check to find out what size and pocket configurations are available before you start to design.*

## TRAY-STYLE CARTONS

A basic type of folding carton is the *tray*, a relatively shallow carton with a bottom hinged to wide side and end walls. The sides and ends are connected by a flap, hook, locking tab, or lock that can be glued, or assembled without glue. Tray cartons can also consist of two pieces, one slightly larger than the other, forming the base and cover of a two-piece telescoping box. Trays are often used for baked goods, cigarettes, for food service items, and as pizza carryout containers.

 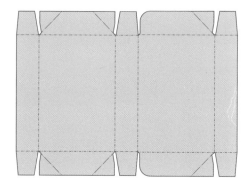

### Six-Point Glued Tray with Integral Lid

Preglued corners provide extra strength and ease of assembly. Structure is erected by pulling out the sides of the tray. Because it stores flat and is easily opened, this type of container works well in the fast-food industry.

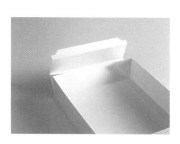 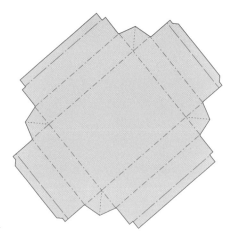

### Web Corner Tray

Easy-erect tray cartons assemble without glue. The diagonal fold across each corner creates a web that's held in place by flaps. An appropriate alternative in situations when gluing isn't an option.

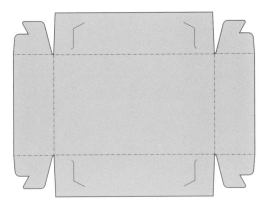

## Corner-Locked Tray

Another option when gluing isn't available is tongue-and-slot corners that are used to form sides. This option is not as rigid as the web corner tray, however it uses less material. This style can be made into a container with a lid by using one tray as the base and a slightly larger one for the lid.

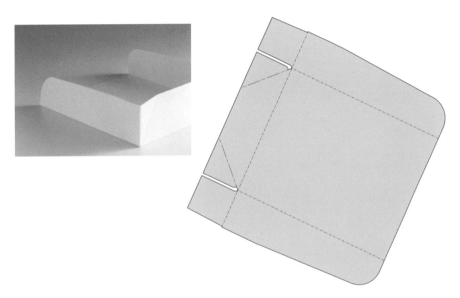

## Open-Ended Tray

Glue-assembled trays are frequently used for baked goods and other food items when display of product is important. Product is protected with shrink-wrap, cellophane, or other transparent wrapping.

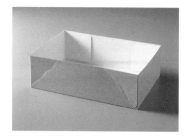

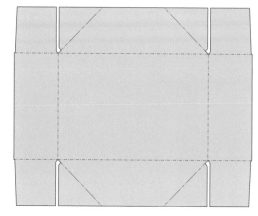

### In-Fold/Out-Fold Tray

Glue-cornered trays store flat and then
self-erect when the sides are lifted. They can be shrink-wrapped when display of product is
important. They can also be formed into a container with a lid by using one tray as the base
and a slightly larger one for the lid in a combination often used for gift boxes.

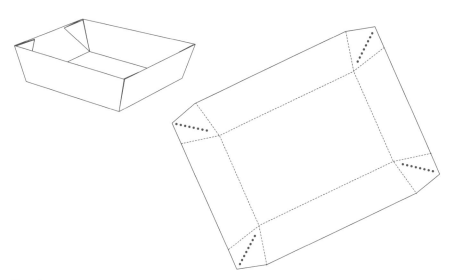

### Glue-Cornered Taper Tray

Preassembled and glued trays stack well and can function equally well as a plate or dish.
they are frequently used in the food service industry for serving french fries, salads, and
other nonliquid products.

## BASIC TUBE-STYLE CARTONS

Tube-style folding cartons are rectangular sleeves formed from a sheet of board that is folded over and glued against its edges. Tubes have openings at the top and bottom that are closed with flaps, reverse, or straight tucks and locks that can be glued or assembled without glue.

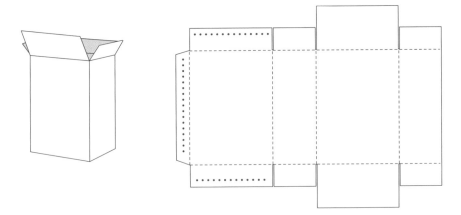

### Skillet or Sealed End Carton

Flaps are sealed using glue or tape. Most shipping cartons use this configuration and closure because it provides the most economical use of carton board.

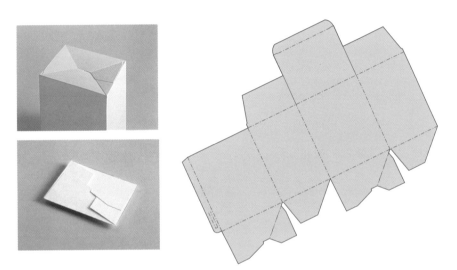

### Tuck-Top Crash Base Carton

Used when fast assembly of the carton is important. Cartons are preglued and folded flat. When opened for assembly, the base slides into position and locks when all sides meet.

## BASIC CLOSURE TYPES

In addition to providing a temporary barrier between the package's contents and the outside, the closure can also contribute to the rigidity of the carton. The closure may also determine or transform the purpose of a carton.

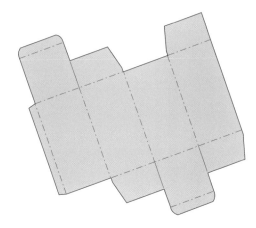

### Standard Tuck-Flap

Appropriate for individually wrapped items such as bandages or products in squeezable tubes. Also a good choice as a container for food items such as tea and sugar packets where reusability is important. May require a seal or outer wrapping to ensure contents will remain intact prior to purchase.

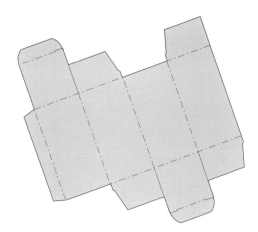

### Slit-Lock Tuck

Applications are similar to standard tuck-flap carton, except slits provide a more secure seal. For tamper resistance, add a seal or a protective outer wrapping.

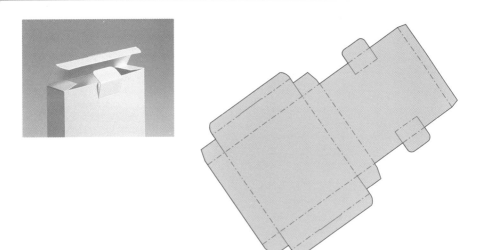

**Tab Lock**
Slits and tab provide additional protection against tampering and lid being forced open by inside pressure from the contents.

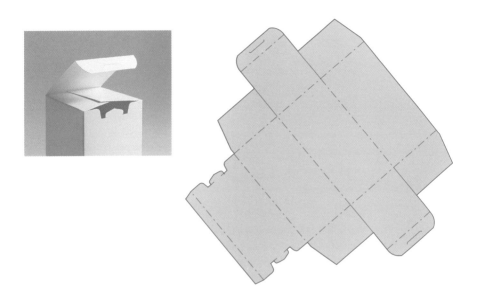

**Postal Lock**
Although not reusable, this completely tamper-proof option has an arrowhead tab that tears on opening, providing proof of entry.

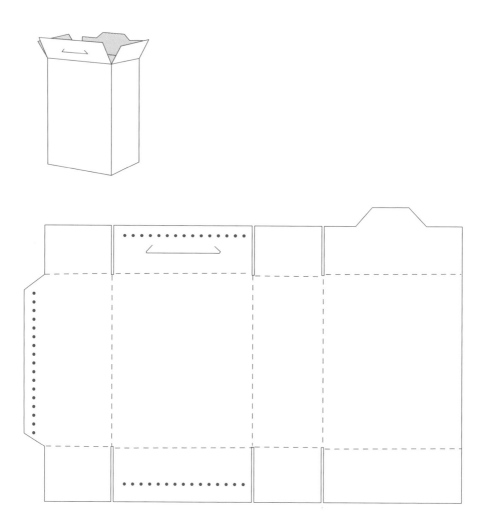

**Partial Overlap Seal End with Lock Tab and Lock Slot**

This closure option is appropriate for items contained in an interior, moisture-proof pouch including cereal, cookies, or crackers. The top is often glued shut to prevent tampering prior to purchase, leaving the tab and slot as a reusable closure after the carton is opened.

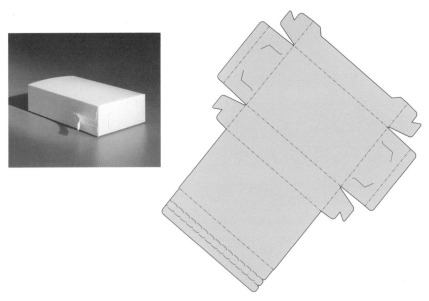

### Pull-Strip or Zipper Carton

Commonly used to prevent tampering. The pull-strip provides an irreversible method of opening. Suitable for cereals, crackers, and other foods contained in an interior, moisture-proof pouch. Note: All flaps must be glued or have locking closures to prevent access via another entrance and to ensure pull-strip will be properly aligned.

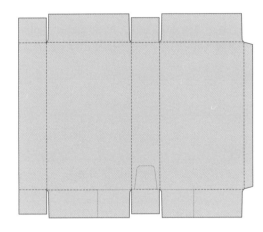

### Pour-Spout Container

Score lines along the container's top and side allow the consumer to access the product and pour the contents in a controlled manner. This type of carton is commonly used for cereal and detergent.

## FOLDERS, SLEEVES, AND OTHER TYPES OF FOLDING CARTONS

These packaging options suit the needs of specialty packaging and specific products.

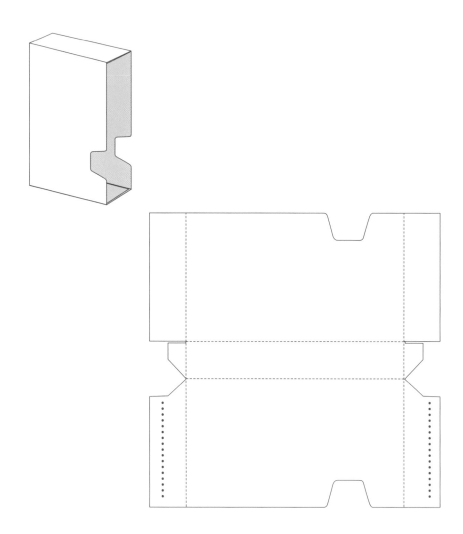

### Open-End Sleeve with Finger Holes

Finger holes and open-end construction allow easy access to videotape cassettes.

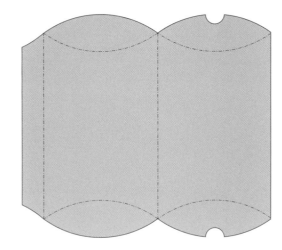

## Pillow Pack

Functions well for packaging soft items such as clothing or a number of small pieces. Easily erectable and can be stored in flat-packed state. Package design can also be easily modified to a pull-strip closure.

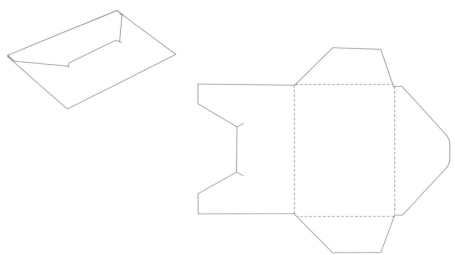

## Shallow Folder

This type of package makes economical use of resources for packaging flat items such as hosiery. Its tuck-in closure can be sealed or replaced with a pull-strip to make the container tamper resistant.

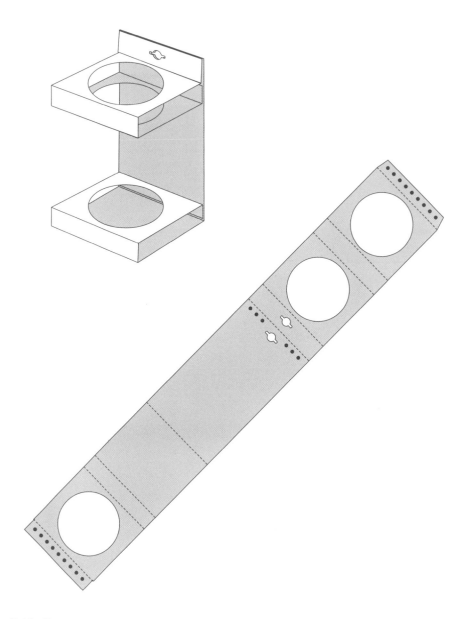

**Bottle Hanger**
This one-piece construction lends itself to a variety of lightweight, cylindrical items and provides maximum product visibility.

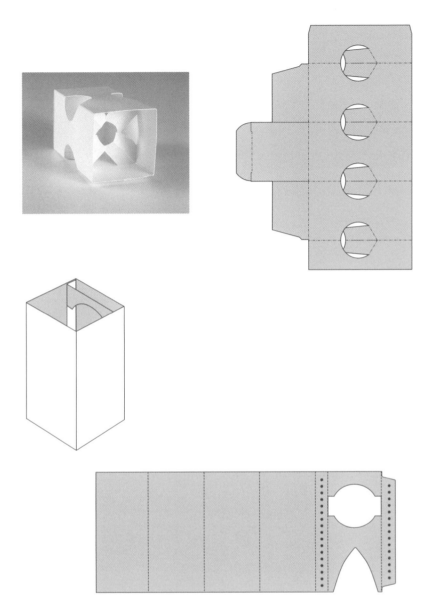

**Lightbulb Sleeve**

These designs use inner panels and die cuts to protect and immobilize lightbulbs.
The design can be modified to suit similarly fragile products.

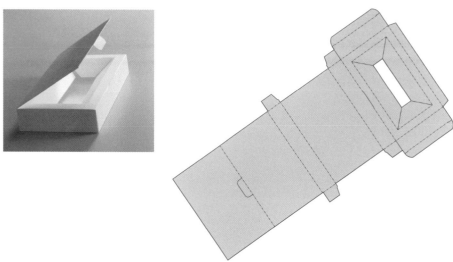

**Display Carton**

The extended lid flap on this carton opens to reveal a display recess to accommodate a product. Cut from a single sheet, this design only requires one side of the board to be printed.

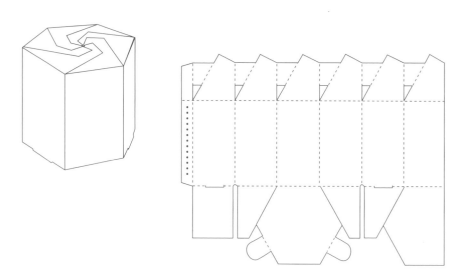

**Six-Sided Carton with Push-in Closure**

The small triangles have been die-cut out of the top closure to permit easier closing. Assembly requires glue on the side but not on the bottom of the carton. Suitable for novelty and gift items.

## SET-UP BOXES

Set-up or rigid paper boxes are assembled by piecing together flat sheets of boxboard, which are held together at the sides with corner stays and adhesive. The assembled box is covered with decorative paper that is adhered to the exterior surface. Unlike folding cartons, which are often delivered flat, set-up boxes are delivered as a three-dimensional product ready to be filled with merchandise. They can be easily adapted to a variety of applications that may include platforms, plastic domes, or compartments. Their decorative quality makes them suitable for cosmetics, candy, and jewelry. Set-up boxes instantly add an upscale look to gifts, gift boxes, and luxury items.

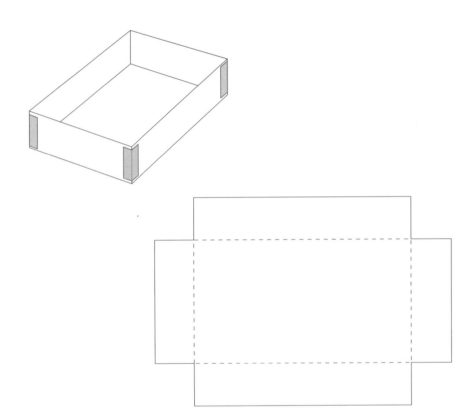

### Basic Set-up Construction

A simple set-up box involves scoring a sheet of box board so that the sides can be folded at right angles to the base. The side panels are fastened at the corners with tape, fabric, or metal. The assembled box is covered with a precut sheet of paper that is scored at the fold lines, adhered to the outside, and wrapped around the box edges so that it covers a portion of the interior. Two trays, such as the one shown here, are typically combined to form a box and lid.

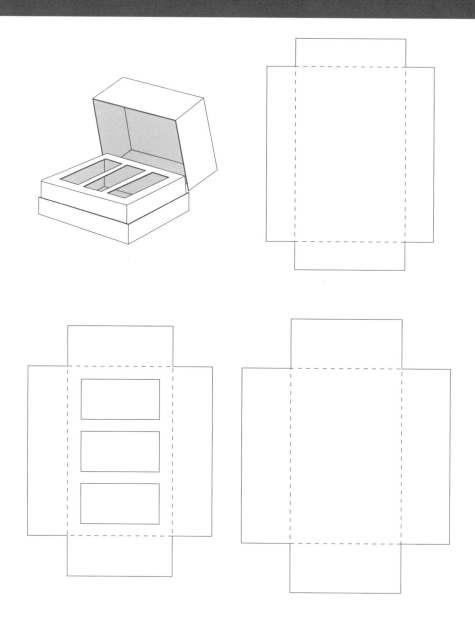

## Lidded Box with Raised Platform

Boxes with raised platforms work well as a means of showcasing watches, jewelry, or other valuables. The platform openings can be replaced with slits for displaying rings or adapted in other ways, depending on the shape of the objects inside.

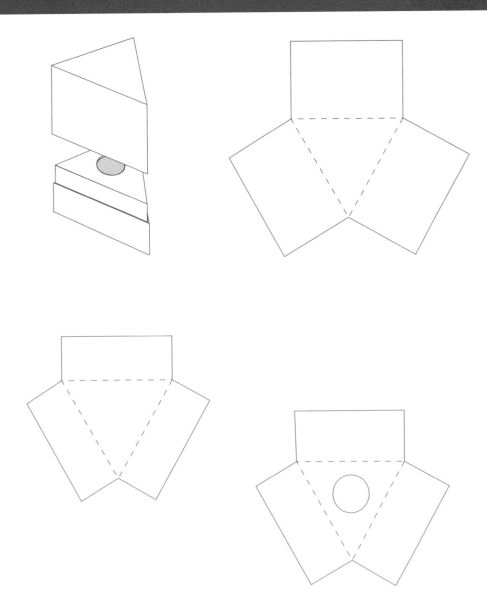

**Triangular Box with Raised Platform**

This alternative to the standard, four-sided box makes an unusual presentation. The deep lid makes this construction suitable for a perfume bottle or other vertical container.

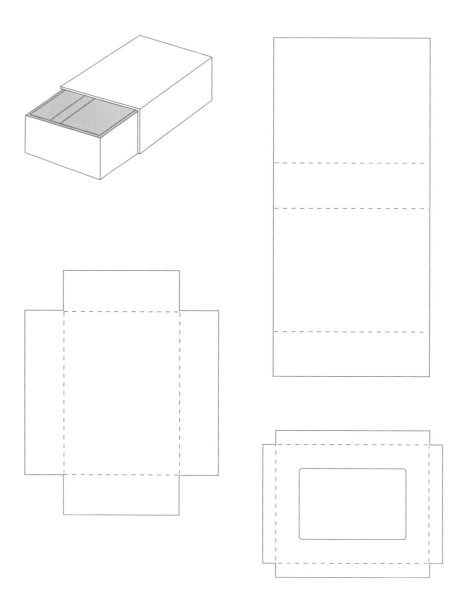

**Tube and Slide**

Without the platform, the tube and slide construction functions much like a matchbox as a container for loose items.

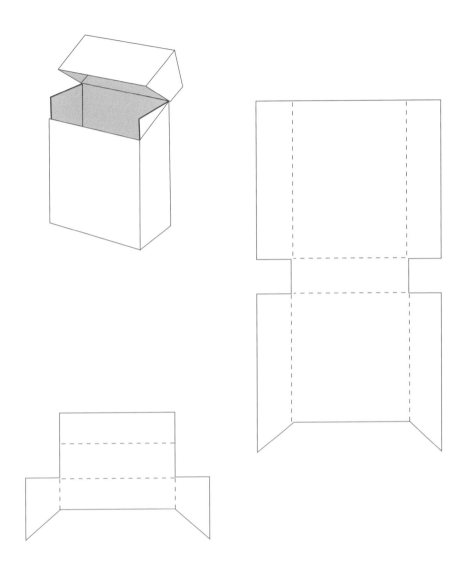

**Hinged-Lid Box**

The vertical nature of this box makes it an ideal container for chalk, crayons, discs, or as a document holder.

## COMMON STYLES OF STOCK PLASTIC CONTAINERS

Plastic containers are generally categorized according to shape: oblong, oval, round, or square. From there, shapes vary according to function. Consult the following diagrams for an overview of some common shapes. Check with specific manufacturers for more specific information on capacity range, container materials, and barrier capabilities.

Classic Oblong

Vanity Oblong

Sprayer: Oblong

Angle Neck Oblong

Lexington Round

Regular Cylinder

Handleware: Slant

Handleware: 2-Gal. Oblong

Sprayer: Pistol Grip

Wide-Mouth Oblong

Straight-Sided Oval

Tapered Oval

Syrup Oval

Boston Round

Bullet Round

Wide-Mouth Square

Carafe: Modern

Handleware: 1-Gal. Round

Jar: Wide-Mouth Round

**GENERAL MAIL CLASSIFICATIONS AND REQUIREMENTS (UNITED STATES)**

The United States Postal Service (USPS) offers many types of mailing services, depending on the nature and size of what you are mailing. To check rates and requirements for your mailing, you must first determine whether your piece fits the description of a letter, a large envelope, or a package and whether or not your piece fits within the size requirements for each.

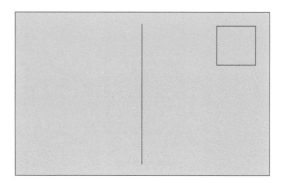

**Postcard**
Rectangular cardstock mail piece not contained within an envelope.

**Letter**
Small, rectangular mail piece.

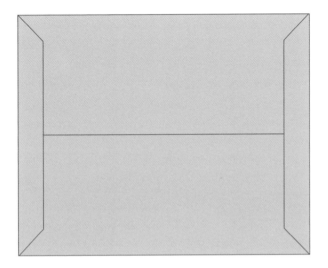

**Large envelope or flat**
Flat, rectangular mail piece.

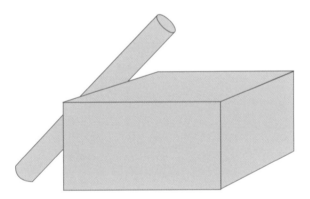

**Package**
A three-dimensional mail piece contained in a box, thick envelope, or tube.

## Size Requirements for Flat Mail (United States)

USPS rates are based on mail that is automation compatible. Nonautomation compatible mail pieces that do not comply with size and aspect ratio (width to height ratio) requirements are assessed a surcharge. These are the size requirements for automated processing of flat mail. If your piece does not fall within these dimensions, check with a USPS agent to see what the mailing cost will be. (The standards and requirements listed are current at the time of publication. Check with a postal agent or the USPS website at www.USPS.com for updates.)

| Type | Min./Max | Length | Height |
|---|---|---|---|
| Postcards* | Minimum | 5 inches (127 mm) | 3 $1/2$ inches (89 mm) |
| | Minimum | 7 inches (178 mm) | 4 $1/4$ inches (108 mm) |
| Letter | Minimum | 5 inches (127 mm) | 3 $1/2$ inches (89 mm) |
| | Minimum | 11 $1/2$ inches (292 mm) | 6 $1/8$ inches (155 mm) |
| Large envelope or flat | Minimum | 11 $1/2$ inches (292 mm) | 6 $1/8$ inches (156 mm) |
| | Minimum | 15 $3/4$ inches (400 mm) | 12 inches (305 mm) |

*Postcards larger than the maximum size allowed qualify as "flats."

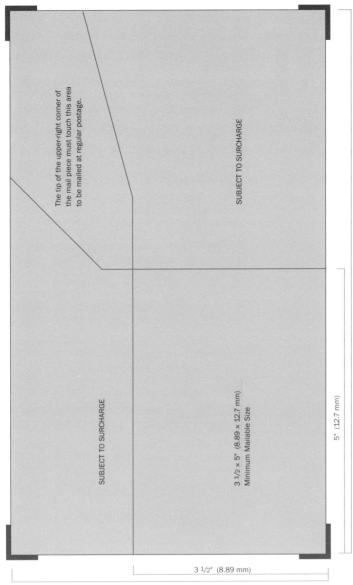

The tip of the upper-right corner of the mail piece must touch this area to be mailed at regular postage.

SUBJECT TO SURCHARGE

SUBJECT TO SURCHARGE

3 1/2 x 5" (8.89 x 12.7 mm)
Minimum Mailable Size

11 1/2" (29.21 mm)
Maximum Standard Length

5" (12.7 mm)

3 1/2" (8.89 mm)

6 1/8" (15.5575 mm)
Maximum Standard Length

Off-size, square envelopes, and mail not complying with the USPS's mailing standards are subject to a surcharge. Refer to this template to determine if your piece falls within the USPS's guidelines for proper size and aspect ratio. (Scale of diagram is 50% of original size.)

## Thickness Requirements for Flat Mail (United States)

The USPS also has requirements for the thickness of cards, envelopes, and flats.

*Letter envelopes:* Must be $1/4$ inch (6.35 mm) or less in thickness.

*Large envelopes or flats:* Must be 0.009 inch (0.2286 mm) and no more than $3/4$ inch (19.05 mm) in thickness.

*Postcards:* Cards measuring 4 $1/4$ x 6" (10.795 mm x 15.25 mm) or less must be printed on stock that is at least 0.007 inch (0.1778mm) or a basis weight of at least 75#. Postcards larger than 4 $1/4$ x 6" (10.795 mm x 15.25 mm) must have a thickness of 0.009 inch (0.2286 mm) or a basis weight of at least 80#.

## Size Requirements for Packages (United States)

Merchandise, catalogs, tubes, and other items not meeting the description of a letter, postcard, or a flat are categorized as either bound printed material (books, catalogs, and other publications) or packages. Publications must not exceed 15 lb. (6.804 kg) per unit. Packages must not exceed 70 lb. (31.752 kg) or measure more than 130 inches (330.2 mm) in combined length and distance around the thickest part.

If your package weighs less than 1 lb. (0.4536 kg) you can drop it into a collection box. Anything over this weight must be handed to your letter carrier or taken to a post office.

## Rate Classifications and Delivery Time for Domestic Mail (United States)

USPS mailing services are classified by type of mailing and delivery time. Bulk discounts are also available. The following is a list of basic rate classifications and the delivery options available within each. (The services and their requirements listed below are current at the time of publication. Check with a postal agent or the USPS website at www.usps.com for updates.)

LETTERS, POSTCARDS, PERIODICALS

*Express:* Premium delivery service provides guaranteed one- to two-day delivery for documents that will fit within USPS Express envelopes. Pricing is calculated on weight and distance. Signature proof of delivery and tracking is available.

*Priority:* Ensures an average two- to three-day delivery for packages up to 70 lb. (31.752 kg) and measuring up to 108 inches (2743 mm) in combined length and distance around the thickest part. Pricing is calculated on weight and distance.

*First Class Mail:* Used primarily for correspondence, this option is available for letters, envelopes, and postcards weighing 13 ounces (368.5435 gm) or less. Delivery is ensured within one to three days.

*Periodical Mail:* Newspapers, magazines, and newsletters qualify for this discounted rate with an average of one- to seven-day delivery. No special services are available for this option.

*Business Reply Mail:* This service lets the sender pay for the recipient's response by establishing an account that covers their mailing costs. Users pay an annual fee, receive a permit, a permit number, and pay an additional amount for each response they receive.

**Bulk Rate:** Discounted rates are available for large mailings with an average two- to nine-day delivery within the continental U.S. Presorting and other preparatory work is required, as well as a permit number and an annual mailing fee. Minimums and size requirements vary depending on the pieces being mailed.

- Standard Mail: A minimum of 200 pieces or 50 lb. (22.68 kg) per mailing is required. Pieces must weigh less than 16 ounces (453.592 gm).

- First Class Mail: A minimum of 500 pieces per mailing is required. Pieces must meet size and weight requirements for first class mail: Up to 13 ounces (368.543 gm).

- Parcel Post: A minimum of 50 pieces per mailing is required. Pieces must meet size and weight requirements for Parcel Post: Up to 130 inches (3302 mm) combined length and distance around the thickest part; up to 70 lb. (31.752 kg).

- Presorted Library Mail: A minimum of 300 pieces is required. Pieces must meet size and weight requirements for Library Mail: Up to 108 inches (2743 mm) combined length and distance around the thickest part; up to 70 lb. (31.752 kg).

- Presorted Media Mail: A minimum of 300 pieces is required. Pieces must meet size and weight requirements for Media Mail: Up to 108 inches (2743 mm) combined length and distance around the thickest part; up to 70 lb. (31.752 kg).

- Carrier Route Bound Printed Matter: A minimum of 300 pieces is required. Pieces must meet weight requirements for Carrier Route Bound Printed Matter: Up to 40 lb. (18.144 kg).

## PACKAGES

**Bound Printed Matter:** Catalogs, directories, and other permanently bound sheets of promotional or editorial material qualify for this rate category. Delivery ranges two to nine days. Weight limit is up to 15 lb. (6.804 kg) per piece.

**Library Rate:** Special, discounted rate for educational groups, nonprofit organizations, and other qualifying institutions.

**Media Mail (also called Book Rate):** Cost-efficient way to mail books, sound recordings, video tapes, printed music as well as CDs, DVDs, and diskettes. Media mail cannot contain advertising. Weight limit is up to 70 lb. (31.752 kg). Delivery ranges from two to nine days.

**Parcel Post:** Includes boxes, tubes, and rolls. Most economic option for mailing small and large packages weighing up to 70 lb. (31.752 kg) and measuring up to 130 inches (330.2 mm) in combined length and distance around the thickest part.

**Parcel Select:** Discounted rate for large volumes of package shipments.

## Rate Classifications and Delivery Time for International Mail

These rates and delivery times apply to international mail. (The services and their requirements listed below are current at the time of publication. Check with a postal agent or the USPS website at www.usps.com for updates.)

*Global Express Guaranteed:* Guaranteed delivery within two to three days to more than 200 countries. Pricing is calculated on weight and distance. Signature, proof of delivery, and tracking are available.

*Global Express Mail:* Delivery within three to five days to more than 190 countries. Return receipt and tracking are available.

*Global Priority Mail:* Economical option offers delivery within four to six days to 51 countries. Limited to envelopes and packages weighing 4 lb. (1.8144 kg).

## Extra USPS Services

The USPS also offers a range of services that can be added on at an additional cost to the basic cost of mailing a letter or package:

*COD (Collect on Delivery):* Allows the postal service to collect the postage and price of an item from the recipient and give it to the mailer. The addressee must order the goods.

*Certified Mail:* Provides proof of mailing at time of mailing and the date and time of delivery or attempted delivery. Return receipt can be added to confirm delivery.

*Delivery Confirmation:* Provides the date and time of delivery or attempted delivery.

*Signature Confirmation:* Provides the date and time of delivery or attempted delivery.

*Registered Mail:* Provides maximum security. Includes proof of mailing at time of mailing and the date and time of delivery or attempted delivery. Insurance up to $25,000 can be added. Return receipt can be added to confirm delivery.

*Insured Mail:* Provides coverage against loss or damage up to $5,000.

*Return Receipt:* Provides a postcard with the date of delivery and recipient signature. Must be combined with another extra service. Return receipt for merchandise service is also available.

*Certificate of Mailing:* Provides evidence of mailing.

*Return Receipt for Merchandise:* Provides a postcard with the date of delivery and recipient signature. Must be combined with another extra service.

## Label Standards for Automated Mailing (United States)

Bulk mailing of envelopes, postcards, and flats can be discounted if they are prepared according to USPS automation standards. Pieces qualifying for automation rates need to meet specific addressing, bar coding, and design standards.

*Bar codes:* To receive automation rates for cards letters, as well as bulk discounts for parcel post, bound printed matter, and media mail, all the pieces in a mailing must have a delivery point bar code. Automation rate flats must have a delivery point bar code or a ZIP + four bar code. Each piece in a bar coded parcel mailing must have a five-digit bar code. All bar codes must meet placement, size, and legibility standards. Software is available for printing bar coded address labels from a mailing list.

*Address printing:* Dark, nonmetallic ink colors must be printed against a white or pastel background to provide adequate print contrast between the printed address and its background. If necessary, areas of dark solid color on a mail piece must be left color free in the address area. To prevent smearing of printed addresses, the USPS recommends using quick-drying inks on a paper stock with a nonshiny (low gloss) surface. If gloss varnish is applied, a varnish-free zone should be reserved for the address area. Addresses should be not be slanted (or skewed) more than 5 degrees relative to the bottom edge of the mail piece.

```
#XXXXXXX****3-DIGIT 777
JANE PUBLIC
OCEAN PARK DRIVE
ANYTOWN TX 77777-0000
```

Bar coded address label for a postcard, letter, or flat.

```
JANE PUBLIC
OCEAN PARK DRIVE
ANYTOWN TX 77777-0000
                    ZIP 77777
```

Bar coded address label for a package.

```
MR & MRS JOHN A SAMPLE
5505 W SUNSET BLVD APT 230
HOLLYWOOD, CA 90028-8521
```

```
MRS MILDRED DOE
BRAKE CONTROL DIVISION
BIG BUSINESS INCORPORATED
12 E BUSINESS LN STE 209
KRYTON TN 38188-0002
```

Basic address label requirements and quality standards for automated mailings.

## Business Reply and Courtesy Reply Mail (United States)

Business Reply (when the permit holder pays postage) and Courtesy Reply Mail (when the sender pays postage) requires a permit number and special envelope or postcard requirements. Art is supplied by the USPS for the indicia (where the permit number appears with Postage Paid), FIM (facing identification mark) and horizontal bars, if applicable. Because placement standards for these elements are very stringent, the USPS recommends that you submit samples of your mail piece to a mail piece design analyst early in the design process to allow time for changes before printing.

### MAIL PIECE DESIGN EXPERTISE

*Every major U.S. city has a USPS Mail Piece Design Analyst (MPA) on staff to advise on properly designing postcards, envelopes, and packages. MPAs can help you prevent problems before they occur by providing specific recommendations on samples of a mail piece during the design process. They can also offer suggestions at the onset of a project for the most cost-efficient design and mailing option. MPAs also hold regular seminars that are open to the business community at no charge. To locate your regional MPA, contact the main USPS post office branch in your area.*

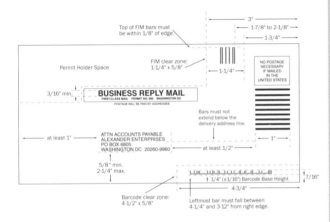

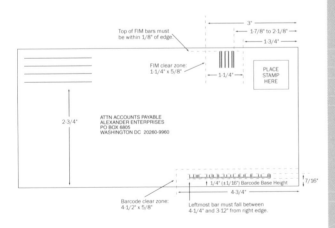

Elements that appear on the face of a Business Reply Mail or Courtesy Reply postcard or envelope must be positioned as shown above.

## Sealing Self-Mailers (United States)

Folded self-mailers need to be sealed in way that allows them to be easily fed through the USPS's automated equipment. Consult the diagrams that follow to determine where wafer seals and tabs should be placed.

Double Postcard Size

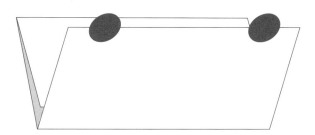

Folded Self-Mailer

Multiple-Sheet Mailer

Short-Fold Mailer

Invitation-Fold Mailer

Booklet with Cover

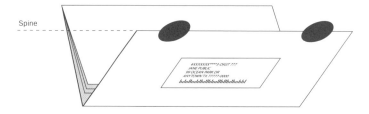

Folded Booklet 1

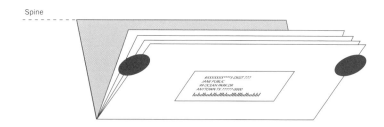

Folded Booklet 2

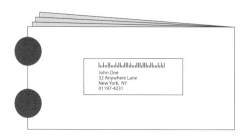

Short-Fold Booklet

## Postal Websites

Because postal regulations and rates are constantly changing, these websites can help keep you up to date on mailing procedures, current rates and regulations, as well as a rate calculator and other features. Some sites allow users to track mailings, download publications, and print labels.

GENERAL

### Universal Postal Union

www.upu.int/
The Universal Postal Union is a department within the United Nations that coordinates worldwide postal services.

### Post Info

www.postinfo.net
This website is dedicated to international mailing information providing links to international postal authorities.

INTERNATIONAL POSTAL SERVICE WEBSITES

### Åland
Åland Post
www.posten.aland.fi/start_en.asp

### Argentina
Correo Argentino
www.correoargentino.com.ar/

### Ascension Island
Ascension Island Post Office and Philatelic Bureau
www.postoffice.gov.ac/

### Australia
Australia Post
www.auspost.com.au/

### Austria
Austrian Poastal Services- PTA-Post and Telekom Austria
www.pta.at/

### Belgium
De Post - La Poste - Die Post
www.post.be/

### Bermuda
Bermuda General Post Office
www.bermudapostoffice.com/

### Brazil
Correios (Postal Administration of Brazil)
www.correios.com.br/

### Brunei Darussalam
Brunei Postal Services Department
www.post.gov.bn/

### Bulgaria
Bulgarian Posts
www.bgpost.bg/

### Cambodia
Ministry of Posts
www.mptc.gov.kh/

### Canada
Canada Post / Postes Canada
www.canadapost.ca

### Channel Islands
Guernsey Post Limited
www.guernseypost.com/

### Chile
Correos de Chile
www.correos.cl/

### China
China Post
chinapost.gov.cn/english/

### Costa Rica
Correos de Costa Rica
www.correos.go.cr/CORREOSWEB
    SITE_ingles/index_in.html

### Croatia
Hvratska Posta
www.posta.hr/

### Czech Republic
Ceska Posta
www.cpost.cz/

**Denmark**
Post Danmark
www.postdanmark.dk/

**Estonia**
Eesti Post
www.post.ee/

**Faroe Islands**
Postverk Føroya
www.stamps.fo

**Fiji**
Post Fiji
www.postfiji.com.fj/

**Finland**
Suomen Posti Oy
www.posti.fi/

**France**
La Poste française
www.laposte.fr

**French Polynesia**
Philatelic Center
www.tahiti-postoffice.com

**Germany**
Deutsche Post
www.deutschepost.de/postagen/

**Greece**
Hellenic Post
www.elta-net.gr

**Honduras**
Correos de Honduras
www.honduras.net/honducor/index.html

**Hong Kong**
Hongkong Post
www.hongkongpost.com/

**Hungary**
Posta
www.posta.hu/

**Iceland**
Íslandspóstur
www.postur.is/

**Ireland**
An Post
www.anpost.ie/

**Isle of Man Post**
Isle of Man Post
www.iompostoffice.com/

**Jamaica**
Postal Corporation of Jamaica Ltd
www.jamaicapost.gov.jm/

**Japan**
Postal Services Agency
www.yusei.go.jp/eng/english/english
    index.html

**Jordan**
Jordan Ministry of Post and
Communications
www.mopc.gov.jo/

**Kazakhstan**
Kazpost
www.kazpost.kz/kazpost_e.html

**Kenya**
Postal Corporation of Kenya
www.posta.co.ke/

**Latvia**
Latvijas pasts / Latvia Post
www.post.lv/

**Lesotho**
Lesotho Postal Services
www.lps.org.ls/

**Lithuania**
Lithuania Post
www.post.lt/

**Luxembourg**
P and T Luxembourg–Postes
www.postes.lu/

**Mauritius**
Ministry of Information Technology &
Telecommunications–Postal Services
Division
ncb.intnet.mu/mitt/postal/index.htm

**Netherlands Antilles**
Post Netherlands Antilles
www.postna.com/

**New Zealand**
New Zealand Post
www.nzpost.co.nz/

**Nicaragua**
Correos de Nicaragua
www.correos.com.ni/

**Norway**
Posten
www.posten.no/

**Pakistan**
Pakistan Post
www.pakpost.gov.pk/

**Philippines**
Philippine Postal Corporation
www.philpost.gov.ph/

**Pitcairn Island**
Pitcairn Island Mail & Stamps
www.lareau.org//pitmail.html

**Poland**
Poczta Polska
www.poczta-polska.pl/

**Portugal**
Correios de Portugal
www.ctt.pt/

**Republic of Cyprus**
Cyprus Postal Services
www.pio.gov.cy/dps/index.html

**Republic of Maldives**
Maldives Post Ltd
www.maldivespost.com/

**Saint Helena**
The Island of St. Helena Post Office and
Philatelic Bureau
www.postoffice.gov.sh/

**Singapore**
Singapore Post
www.singpost.com.sg/

**Slovakia**
Slovenska Posta
www.slposta.sk/

**South Africa**
South African Post Office
www.sapo.co.za/

**Sweden**
Sweden Post
www.posten.se/

**Switzerland**
La Poste - La Posta - Die Post
www.post.ch

**Tanzania**
Tanzania Posts Corporation
www.tanpost.com/

**Thailand**
Communications Authority of Thailand
www.cat.or.th/

**Ukraine**
Ukrainian Post Home Page
www.ukrposhta.com/

**United Kingdom**
Royal Mail
www.royalmail.co.uk

British Forces Post Office
www.bfpo.org.uk/

Royal Mail
www.royalmail.com/
*Includes a finder for postcodes and Post
Office.*

Post Office Reform
www.dti.gov.uk/postalservices/network.htm
*News and information on the changes
being brought about in the postal market*

**United States**
The United States Postal Service
www.USPS.com

# Chapter 11: Bar Code Standards

## GENERAL STANDARDS FOR UPC BAR CODES

Bar codes are a series of horizontal or vertical parallel lines representing a code that can be optically read and interpreted by a bar code scanner. Bar coding is used on packaging to speed up pricing at checkout.

- Bar codes must be positioned in a spot that is highly visible and easy to be scanned.

- A bar code must be printed at a scale between 85% and 120% of its original size.

- Bar codes must be printed in dark colors (dark shades or blue black and brown or black) against a solid light colored background. (See the following section, Guide to Color Correct Bar Coding, for more specific information on which colors are readable when printed on common paperboard surfaces.)

- Bars must be printed in a solid color, not screen values of spot colors or screened blends of process colors.

- Bar codes against a colored field must have a color-free area that extends no less than $3/32$ inch beyond the printed bar code.

- To guard against ink spread, bars should run vertically across the rollers on a web press.

1 ⅛" (1.125") (29 mm)

1 ⁹/₃₂" (1.59375") (41 mm)

100% NOMINAL
Minimum Free Space

## Guide to Color-Correct Bar Coding

The key to printing a bar code that can be optically scanned is selecting a color that contrasts sufficiently with its background that the scanner can distinguish between the bars and the background. Coming up with the right combination means checking the background reflectance value of your substrate and combining it with an ink color that contrasts sufficiently.

These are the reflectance values of some common papers. The lighter the color, the higher its reflectance value:

| Substrate | Reflectance Value (%) |
|-----------|----------------------|
| Natural Kraft | 26–43 |
| Mottled | 56–77 |
| Bleached | 77–87 |

Inks have a reflectance value as well. Darker colors have a lower reflectance value than lighter colors. To see if the reflectance value of your ink color is low enough to contrast with the substrate on which it will be printed, check its reflectance value and compare it with the reflectance value of your substrate. The tables below list substrate reflectance values in column A and ink reflectance values in column B for UPC and EAN bar codes. Find the reflectance value of your substrate in column A and read across to column B to find the maximum reflectance value of your ink color. Example: If your substrate is natural kraft with a reflectance value of 31%, the reflectance value of your ink must be 2.5% or less. (A chart listing reflectance values of common CMYK colors follows this section.)

### TABLE 1: UPC VERSIONS A&E AND EAN 8 & 13*

| Column A | Column B |
|----------|----------|
| Background Reflectance (%) | Ink Reflectance (%) |
| 31.6 | 2.5 |
| 35 | 3.3 |
| 40 | 4.6 |
| 45 | 6.3 |
| 50 | 8.3 |
| 55 | 10.6 |
| 60 | 13.3 |
| 65 | 16.4 |
| 70 | 19.8 |
| 75 | 23.7 |
| 80 | 28.1 |
| 85 | 32.9 |
| 90 | 38.1 |

*Bar codes for U.S. products are designated as UPC versions A and E. Bar codes for European products are designated as EAN 8 and 13. UPC version E and EAN version 13 are small-scale bar codes intended for use on small products or containers such as chapstick.

(Table 1 was excerpted from *The Bar Code Color Book*, a book published by Symbology, Incorporated. Contact Symbology for a more complete guide on color-correct bar code printing, including color reflectance values for PANTONE® colors, at 800-328-2612 (in Minnesota 612-315-8080).

## Reflectance Values of Four-Color Combinations on Uncoated Stock

Because colors with a reflectance value of more than 40 have the potential to create scanning problems on a bright, white substrate, the following list includes colors with a reflectance value of 40 or less. However, if it's important to use a color not on this list, check with your printer to see if there is a possibility of using it for your bar code printing needs. (Note: All reflectance values must be considered accurate plus or minus 5 percent. Ink quality and printing method will affect reflectance values.)

| Color | Reflectance Value (%) | Color | Reflectance Value (%) |
|---|---|---|---|
| 100C, 70M (Reflex Blue) | 3 | 80Y, 100C | 12 |
| 100C (Process Blue) | 4 | 70Y, 20C | 38 |
| 100C, 60Y (Green) | 5 | 70Y, 30C | 32 |
| 100Y, 30K | 40 | 70Y, 40C | 18 |
| 100Y, 40K | 28 | 70Y, 50C | 14 |
| 100Y, 50K | 19 | 70Y, 60C | 14 |
| 100Y, 60K | 16 | 70Y, 70C | 13 |
| 100Y, 20C | 35 | 70Y, 80C | 13 |
| 100Y, 30C | 32 | 70Y, 90C | 12 |
| 100Y, 40C | 15 | 70Y, 100C | 11 |
| 100Y, 50C | 15 | 60Y, 20C | 38 |
| 100Y, 60C | 14 | 60Y, 30C | 32 |
| 100Y, 70C | 14 | 60Y, 40C | 17 |
| 100Y, 80C | 13 | 60Y, 50C | 13 |
| 100Y, 90C | 13 | 60Y, 60C | 11 |
| 100Y, 100C | 13 | 60Y, 70C | 11 |
| 90Y, 20C | 35 | 60Y, 80C | 10 |
| 90Y, 30C | 32 | 60Y, 90C | 10 |
| 90Y, 40C | 28 | 60Y, 100C | 9 |
| 90Y, 50C | 28 | 50Y, 20C | 38 |
| 90Y, 60C | 16 | 50Y, 30C | 30 |
| 90Y, 70C | 15 | 50Y, 40C | 21 |
| 90Y, 80C | 14 | 50Y, 50C | 14 |
| 90Y, 90C | 13 | 50Y, 60C | 9 |
| 90Y, 100C | 13 | 50Y, 70C | 8 |
| 80Y, 30C | 40 | 50Y, 80C | 8 |
| 80Y, 40C | 27 | 50Y, 90C | 7 |
| 80Y, 50C | 21 | 50Y, 100C | 5 |
| 80Y, 60C | 15 | 40Y, 30C | 33 |
| 80Y, 70C | 13 | 40Y, 40C | 30 |
| 80Y, 80C | 13 | P40Y, 50C | 21 |
| 80Y, 90C | 12 | 40Y, 60C | 17 |

| Color | Reflectance Value (%) | Color | Reflectance Value (%) |
|---|---|---|---|
| 40Y, 70C | 8 | 80Y, 100M, 20C | 30 |
| 40Y, 80C | 8 | 60Y, 100M, 30C | 24 |
| 40Y, 90C | 7 | 60Y, 100M, 50C | 14 |
| 40Y, 100C | 5 | 50Y, 90M, 20C | 35 |
| 30Y, 30C | 32 | 50Y, 90M, 40C | 22 |
| 30Y, 40C | 27 | 40Y, 100M, 40C | 26 |
| 30Y, 50C | 20 | 40Y, 100M, 50C | 16 |
| 30Y, 60C | 15 | 30Y, 100M, 30C | 30 |
| 30Y, 70C | 12 | 30Y, 100M, 50C | 17 |
| 30Y, 80C | 7 | 20Y, 100M, 10C | 40 |
| 30Y, 90C | 5 | 20Y, 100M, 30C | 30 |
| 30Y, 100C | 3 | 10Y, 100M, 20C | 38 |
| 20Y, 30C | 37 | 10Y, 100M, 40C | 23 |
| 20Y, 40C | 30 | 100M, 10K | 40 |
| 20Y, 50C | 27 | 100M, 20K | 32 |
| 20Y, 60C | 16 | 100M, 30K | 30 |
| 20Y, 70C | 10 | 100M, 40K | 24 |
| 10Y, 30C | 37 | 100M, 50K | 18 |
| 10Y, 40C | 33 | 100M, 60K | 14 |
| 10Y, 50C | 24 | 100M, 70K | 11 |
| 10Y, 60C | 18 | 100M, 80K | 9 |
| 10Y, 70C | 15 | 90M, 20K | 38 |
| 100Y, 5M, 30K | 31 | 90M, 30K | 31 |
| 100Y, 5M, 40K | 22 | 90M, 40K | 22 |
| 100Y, 20M, 20C | 28 | 90M, 50K | 18 |
| 100Y, 30M, 30C | 30 | 90M, 60K | 12 |
| 100Y, 30M, 50C | 16 | 90M, 70K | 11 |
| 100Y, 40M, 40C | 22 | 90M, 80K | 10 |
| 100Y, 40M, 20C | 31 | 80M, 30K | 32 |
| 100Y, 50M, 20C | 29 | 80M, 40K | 22 |
| 100Y, 50M. 30C | 30 | 80M, 50K | 18 |
| 100Y, 60M, 20C | 34 | 80M, 60K | 12 |
| 100Y, 60M, 30C | 23 | 80M, 70K | 8 |
| 100Y, 60M, 40C | 15 | 70M, 30K | 33 |
| 100Y, 70M, 30C | 24 | 70M, 40K | 23 |
| 100Y, 70M, 40C | 14 | 70M, 50K | 18 |
| 100Y, 80M. 20C | 34 | 70M, 60K | 11 |
| 100Y, 80M, 40C | 19 | 60M, 30K | 35 |
| 80Y, 90M, 40C | 18 | 60M, 40K | 30 |

| Color | Reflectance Value (%) | Color | Reflectance Value (%) |
|---|---|---|---|
| 60M, 50K | 11 | 60M, 50C | 22 |
| 100M, 10C | 38 | 60M, 60C | 13 |
| 100M, 20C | 32 | 60M, 70C | 10 |
| 100M, 30C | 28 | 60M, 80 | 7 |
| 100M, 40C | 18 | 60M, 90C | 5 |
| 100M, 50C | 17 | 60M, 100C | 5 |
| 100M, 60C | 14 | 50M, 30C | 34 |
| 100M, 70C | 12 | 50M, 40C | 28 |
| 100M, 80C | 9 | 50M, 50C | 24 |
| 100M, 90C | 5 | 50M, 60C | 15 |
| 100M, 100C | 4 | 50M, 70C | 10 |
| 90M, 20C | 30 | 50M, 80C | 7 |
| 90M, 30C | 26 | 50M, 90C | 5 |
| 90M, 40C | 22 | 50M, 100C | 4 |
| 90M, 50C | 16 | 40M, 30C | 34 |
| 90M, 60C | 14 | 40M, 40C | 27 |
| 90M, 70C | 11 | 40M, 50C | 23 |
| 90M, 80C | 8 | 40M, 60C | 16 |
| 90M, 90C | 6 | 40M, 70C | 12 |
| 90M, 100C | 4 | 40M, 80C | 11 |
| 80M, 30C | 30 | 40M, 90C | 8 |
| 80M, 40C | 25 | 40M, 100C | 5 |
| 80M, 50C | 15 | 30M, 30C | 36 |
| 80M, 60C | 13 | 30M, 40C | 30 |
| 80M, 70C | 10 | 30M, 50C | 26 |
| 80M, 80C | 7 | 30M, 60C | 19 |
| 80M, 90C | 5 | 30M, 70C | 13 |
| 80M, 100C | 4 | 30M, 80C | 11 |
| 70M, 30C | 33 | 30M, 90C | 8 |
| 70M, 40C | 28 | 30M, 100C | 6 |
| 70M, 50C | 20 | 20M, 30C | 36 |
| 70M, 60C | 13 | 20M, 40C | 30 |
| 70M, 70C | 10 | 20M, 50C | 26 |
| 70M, 80C | 7 | 20M, 60C | 20 |
| 70M, 90C | 4 | 20M, 70C | 14 |
| 70M, 100C | 4 | 20M, 80C | 10 |
| 60M, 30C | 33 | 20M, 90C | 8 |
| 60M, 40C | 28 | 20M, 100C | 6 |

| Color | Reflectance Value (%) | Color | Reflectance Value (%) |
|---|---|---|---|
| 10M, 40C | 35 | 50M, 100C, 30K | 4 |
| 10M, 50C | 25 | 100C, 10Y, 10K | 4 |
| 10M, 70C | 10 | 100C, 10Y, 20K | 4 |
| 10M, 80C | 8 | 100C, 10Y, 40K | 3 |
| 10M, 90C | 7 | 100C, 20Y | 6 |
| 10M, 100C | 6 | 100C, 20Y, 10K | 5 |
| 30C | 39 | 100C, 20Y, 20K | 3 |
| 40C | 31 | 100C, 20Y, 40K | 3 |
| 50C | 25 | 60C, 60Y, 10K | 8 |
| 60C | 18 | 90C, 50Y, 10K | 6 |
| 70C | 15 | 90C, 50Y, 20K | 6 |
| 80C | 12 | 30C, 60Y | 32 |
| 90C | 8 | 100C, 30Y, 10K | 3 |
| 30C, 20K | 32 | 100C, 30Y, 20K | 3 |
| 30C, 40K | 16 | 100C, 30Y, 40K | 3 |
| 30C, 60K | 6 | 100C, 40Y, 10K | 4 |
| 40C, 20K | 30 | 100C, 40Y, 20K | 4 |
| 40C, 40K | 15 | 100C, 50Y, 10K | 4 |
| 40C, 60K | 6 | 100C, 50Y, 20K | 2 |
| 50C, 20K | 28 | 100C, 50Y, 10K | 4 |
| 50C, 40K | 13 | 100C, 50Y, 20K | 4 |
| 50C, 60K | 5 | 40C, 80Y, 30K | 13 |
| 60C, 20K | 27 | 30C, 90Y, 10K | 18 |
| 60C, 40K | 12 | 30C, 90Y, 20K | 18 |
| 60C, 60K | 5 | 30C, 90Y, 30K | 17 |
| 70C, 20K | 26 | 20C, 100Y, 10K | 28 |
| 70C, 40K | 11 | 20C, 100Y, 20K | 23 |
| 70C, 60K | 4 | 30C, 100Y, 10K | 20 |
| 80C, 20K | 25 | 30C, 100Y, 20K | 18 |
| 80C, 40K | 10 | 30C, 100Y, 30K | 17 |
| 80C, 60K | 5 | | |
| 100C, 20K | 3 | | |
| 100C, 40K | 3 | | |
| 100C, 60K | 3 | | |
| 70M, 100C, 10K | 4 | | |
| 70M, 100C, 20K | 3 | | |
| 50M, 100C, 10K | 4 | | |
| 50M, 100C, 20K | 4 | | |

## PAPER BAGS

Paper bags are constructed from a continuous web of paper that is formed into a tube and glued along the overlap to form a seam. The tube is torn to a specified length, frequently against a serrated bar, which gives the bag a saw-toothed edge. The end is folded over and glued to form the bottom. There are three general styles of bag construction: flat, square or pinch bottom, and automatic bottom or self-opening style (SOS).

Flat bags are inexpensive to produce and make economical use of materials. They work well for containing flat items such as cookies or greeting cards.

Square or pinch bottom bags can accommodate bulkier items and work well as shopping bags for single purchases of garments and other lightweight merchandise.

Automatic bottom or self-opening style bags are constructed with a more rigid bottom and are often made of kraft paper to serve as grocery bags or with attached handles to serve as shopping bags.

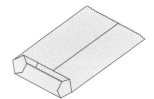

Other styles of bag construction include sewn open-mouth (left) and satchel (right).

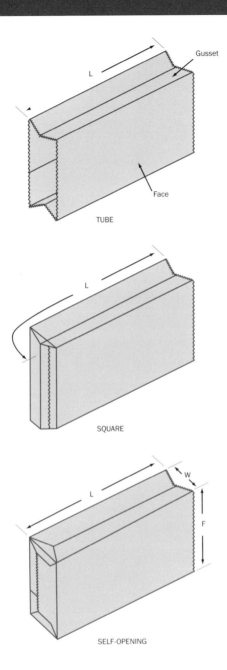

When planning bag construction, dimensions should be specified as face, width (or gusset), and length. Note that length is measured differently for a square (pinch bottom) bag and for a self-opening bag. The length of the tube before it is formed into a bag is sometimes given, and this should not be confused with the finished length (the finishing process reduces the tube length).

## PLASTIC BAGS

Plastic bags are manufactured from plastic tubing or from a flat web that is folded and joined at a back seam. The ends are generally heat sealed to complete the closure.

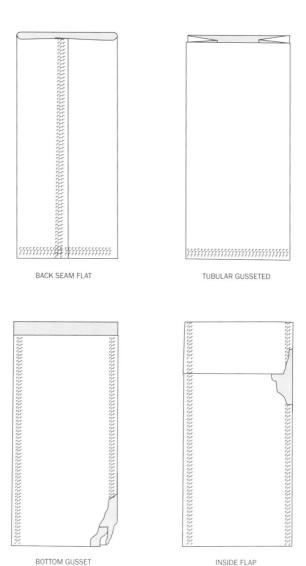

BACK SEAM FLAT

TUBULAR GUSSETED

BOTTOM GUSSET

INSIDE FLAP

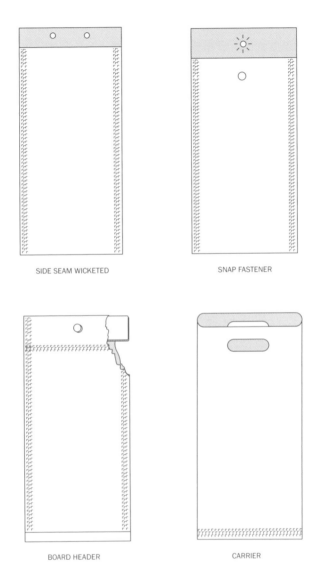

SIDE SEAM WICKETED

SNAP FASTENER

BOARD HEADER

CARRIER

Plastic bags can be manufactured as flat or gusseted and include a variety of styles and closures.

GENERAL GUIDE TO PRINTING PROCESSES

There are many ways of applying ink to paper. The most appropriate option depends on budget, the printing surface, the quantity of the run, and the turnaround time involved. Consult the following list for an overview of the printing methods most commonly available.

*Offset Lithography:* This is the most commonly used method of printing where an image on a plate is "offset" onto a rubber blanket cylinder which, in turn, transfers the image to a sheet of paper. The process is based on making the printing image ink receptive and water repellent, while the nonprinting areas are rendered water receptive and ink repellent. Offset presses may have more than one printing unit, with each delivering a different color. They come in a range of sizes and can accommodate single sheets as well as rolls of paper.

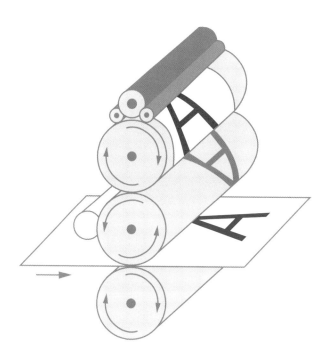

Offset printing involves three rotating cylinders: plate, blanket, and impression. The plate cylinder first contacts the dampening rollers, wetting the plate area. Contact is then made with the inking rollers where the dampened nonimage areas repel the ink. The inked image is then transferred from the plate cylinder to the rubber blanket cylinder. The soft rubber surface of the blanket creates a clear and sharp impression on a range of paper surfaces.

**Letterpress:** One of the oldest and most basic forms of printing, letterpress uses letters molded from lead that are inked and pressed against the paper. Images and graphics can be applied with an etched plate. Text, imagery, and graphics are locked together on the press bed in a "chase." The process typically yields a soft, inked impression on paper. More time intensive than offset, letterpress printing is most often used for printing art books, invitations and announcements, and other situations where an antique or artistic image is desired.

**Gravure:** Web presses are fitted with cylinders that carry an etched plate. The plate transfers the inked, etched image directly onto the paper. Gravure offers excellent image reproduction, but because of the expense involved in plate making, it is usually reserved for extremely large runs such as catalog printing, postage stamps, and packaging applications.

**Engraving:** Similar to gravure, engraving also involves an etched plate that carries an inked impression. With engraving, the paper is positioned and forced against the plate with tremendous pressure, drawing the ink from the depressed areas on the plate and yielding a slightly embossed surface, with a slightly indented impression on the back of the paper. Limit engraved designs to 4 × 9" (101.6 × 228.6 mm), the size of most engraving plates. Engraving yields sharp imagery and text, but the expense involved in plate making makes it suitable for long and repeat runs, such as currency and postage stamps. Engraving is often used when a prestigious, formal look is desired for corporate stationery.

**Thermography:** Similar to engraving in appearance, thermography uses a combination of heat-cured powder and ink to create a raised impression. Thermography costs less than engraving and is often used on business cards and stationery. The process is not appropriate for printing halftones or large areas of color, which are likely to have a pitted or mottled appearance.

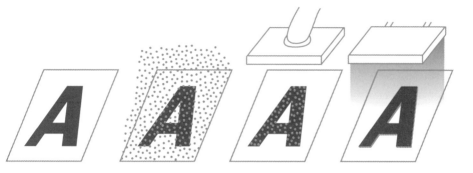

Thermography involves applying powder to a slow-drying ink. After the excess powder is vacuumed away, heat is applied. The curing of the ink and powder causes it to swell, creating a raised impression.

**Screen printing:** A squeegee is pulled across a silk screen to which a stencil has been applied, forcing the ink onto the surface of the paper or substrate. More labor intensive than offset, screen printing is used for printing on surfaces not accommodated on an offset press, such as fabric, industrial papers, acrylic, and metal. The process can be done by hand or by machine. Halftone screens need to be coarse, ranging from 65 to 85 lpi. (See Chapter 4: Imaging and Color for more information on halftone screens.) Often used for printing signage, bottles, garments and other unusual shapes and surfaces.

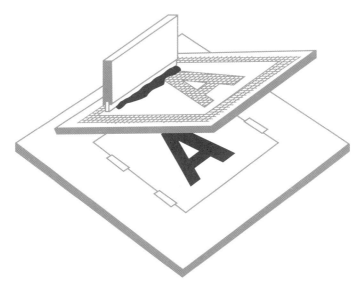

Screen printing involves forcing ink through a mesh screen onto a substrate beneath the screen. The stenciled area on the screen acts as a mask, preventing ink from passing through the nonimage areas of the mesh.

**Flexography:** Web presses are fitted with rubber or soft plastic plates with a raised impression for printing on unusual surfaces not appropriate for offset printing. Substrates include kraft paper, tissue, vinyl, and other types of plastic. Flexography is often used for printing toilet tissue, bread wrappers, plastic bags, and other types of packaging as well as cartons, shopping, and grocery bags.

**Digital:** Often referred to as "on-demand" printing because of its quick turnaround time, digital printing is quickly becoming a viable alternative to traditional offset printing. It is particularly useful for printing short-run (under one thousand) four-color jobs where set-up time and charges would make traditional four-color offset cost prohibitive. The digital process differs from offset in that it is a toner-on-paper process, rather than an ink-on-paper process. Because the color sits on top of the paper, it can flake off at folds or spines. Digital printing also places limitations on sheet sizes, with many presses limited to paper sizes of 11 × 17" (279.4 × 431.8 mm) or less, as well as the types of papers that can be used. When using a digital process, check to see what size and basis weight restrictions may be involved.

*Holography:* Holographic or three-dimensional imagery is created by digitizing an image so that it is divided into several layers. The process involves bouncing laser beams off of mirrors and focusing them onto a photosensitive plate. The holographic design is then embossed onto coated white paper which is metallized for a shimmery effect. Holography requires working closely with specialized vendors over a period of several weeks, and set-up charges can make the process cost-prohibitive for small-run projects. Holography is used on credit cards, trading cards, book covers, beverage packaging, and other situations where high-volume make it a cost-effective option.

*Lenticular printing:* The process creates an animated effect where images flip back and forth when viewed from different angles. (For instance, a photograph of an individual with an eye that actually winks). It is achieved by laminating a plastic lens over two or more images that have been digitized and broken down into a series of dots. Producing a lenticular image requires working closely with a lenticular vendor to produce digital imagery that meets their requirements. The expense and time involved make lenticular printing suitable for mass-production situations such as product manufacture and packaging but unrealistic for small-run or short-turnaround projects.

## TRAPPING TOLERANCES

Keeping colors in register means aligning them on press exactly as they have been specified. But when two colors are adjoining, there is always the possibility that a colorless gap may occur between the colors if registration isn't exact. To compensate for this, a slight overlap, called a *trap,* is created between the two colors. The amount of trapping will vary, depending on the absorbency of the paper or substrate and printing method used. Although most commercial printers take responsibility for creating traps, it's useful to know how trapping tolerances can vary for different printing methods. The following chart shows typical trapping tolerances for a variety of printing processes and substrates:

| Method of Printing | Substrate | Trap (inches) | Trap (mm) | Trap (pt.) |
|---|---|---|---|---|
| Sheetfed offset | uncoated paper | 0.003 | 0.08 | 0.25 |
| Sheetfed offset | coated paper | 0.003 | 0.08 | 0.25 |
| Web offset | coated paper | 0.004 | 0.10 | 0.30 |
| Web offset | uncoated paper | 0.005 | 0.14 | 0.40 |
| Web offset | newsprint paper | 0.006 | 0.15 | 0.45 |
| Gravure | coated paper | 0.003 | 0.08 | 0.25 |
| Flexography | coatedpaper | 0.006 | 0.15 | 0.45 |
| Flexography | newsprint paper | 0.008 | 0.20 | 0.60 |
| Flexography | kraft/corrugated paper | 0.010 | 0.25 | 0.75 |
| Screen printing | fabric | 0 | 0 | 0 |
| Screen printing | paper | 0.006 | 0.15 | 0.45 |

## Types of Offset Lithography

Offset lithography is the most widely used method of printing. The process can be broken down into two basic categories: sheet-fed offset and web offset. Print shops are often set up to specialize in one of these two types of offset printing. Consult the following descriptions for further information on which method is most appropriate for a specific project.

*Sheetfed Offset:* Individual sheets of paper pass through the press. Small, sheetfed presses print on papers smaller than 18 inches (457.2 mm) in width and are used for printing fliers, letterheads, envelopes, and business cards. Larger presses that accommodate paper sizes ranging from 19 × 25" (482.6 × 635 mm) to 55 × 78" (1397 x 1981.2 mm) allow printers to run larger jobs such as posters or book signatures, or gang several pieces on one sheet. Sheetfed presses generally work best for small- to mid-size press runs or when quality is critical.

*Web Offset:* Paper going through a web press is fed from a roll and is cut into sheets after printing. Small-sized web presses that accommodate paper widths of up to 9 inches (228.6 mm) are used for printing business forms and other small pieces. Larger presses (called full web presses) that run rolls from 35 inches to 40 inches (889 to 1016 mm) wide are used for publications. Full web presses can print sixteen page signatures on a trim size that is typically 23 × 35" (635 mm × 889 mm). Web presses are designed to print hundreds of impressions in a minute and many thousands in an hour and are suitable for high-volume publications such as newspapers, magazines, and catalogs. Many presses also come equipped with heating units to speed up ink drying time as well as folding and binding units to expedite production.

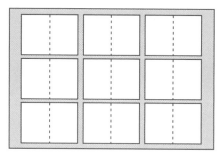

Printers will often gang several pieces on a single sheet, such as fitting nine 4 ½ × 6 ¼" (114 × 159 mm) invitations on a 23 × 35" (584 × 889 mm) sheet of paper.

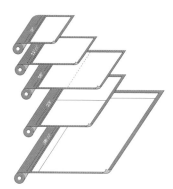

Web presses are categorized according to the size of the paper rolls they run. Small presses called *form webs* are used for business forms, while large presses called *full webs* are used for publications. In-between sizes include miniweb, half web, and ³/₄ web presses.

## Cutting and Trimming

Because most pressruns use paper slightly larger than the finished piece or gang several pieces on a single sheet, waste must be cut away and pieces cut apart. All straight line cuts are called *trims*. Trim lines are indicated by crop marks so that whoever is trimming the job will know where pieces needed to be cut. Trimming a job is included in the cost of printing, and is not the same as perforating, making die-cuts, drilling, or punching holes. These applications are performed at an additional charge. For more information on perforating, die-cuts, drilling and punching, see Finishing Techniques.

## Finishing Techniques

Finishing techniques are applied after a job is printed to create a special effect that can't be achieved with ink. They also include special cuts and trims that are part of the design or applications that make a piece easy to fold, tear, or ready for binding.

*Embossing:* Paper is pressed between two molds called *dies*, typically made from magnesium or brass. The molding of the paper between the dies results in a raised impression. If an impression is molded so that it is lower than the paper's surface, it is called a *deboss*. Embossing can be combined with a printed image or foil stamping to enhance the three-dimensional appearance of the image. An embossed impression made independent of a printed or foil-stamped image is called a *blind emboss*. Soft, uncoated papers generally take a better embossed impression than hard or smooth coated papers. Papers with a textured finish are often preferred because they render a smooth impression that contrasts favorably with the surrounding texture. Text and light- to-mid cover weight stocks work best. Lightweight bonds and writing papers tend to be too thin to show off an emboss, whereas, heavier cover weight stocks can be too thick to be molded. Embossing is frequently used on brochure covers, stationery, business cards, and pocket folders.

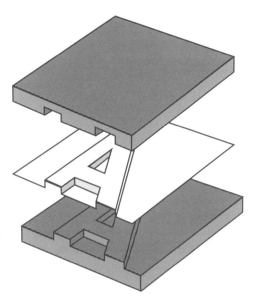

Embossing requires two matched dies (male and female counterparts). One of the dies is heated as the paper is pressed between, resulting in a raised impression.

**Foil stamping:** Paper is stamped with a hot die that presses a thin plastic film carrying colored pigment against the paper. Plastic film comes in more than two hundred colors, including pearlized effects and metallics, as well as clear foil stamps that mimic the look of a varnish. Because the process can render a completely opaque image, foil stamping is often used to apply a light-colored image against a dark-colored paper. In addition to applications on any paper that can withstand heat, foil stamping is also suitable for pens and pencils, cloth book covers, vinyl binders, toys, and other nonpaper applications. When foil stamping is combined with embossing, it's called *foil embossing*. The process involves applying foil first and then the emboss.

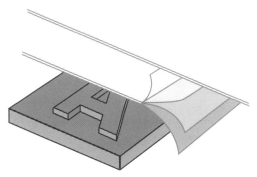

Foil stamping involves applying foil to paper with a heated die. The pigment bonds with the paper, rendering a smooth image.

**Die-cutting:** The process includes making cuts in a printed sheet in a configuration that will allow it to be used or assembled into a functional piece, such as a door hanger, pocket folder, or carton. Die-cutting also includes cuts that enhance a piece's design appeal, such as die-cutting a holiday greeting card in the shape of a Christmas tree. Dies are typically made from bending metal strips with a sharpened edge into the desired shape and mounting them onto a wooden block. The metal strips, called *rules*, are higher than the wooden backing, creating a cutting edge that works much like a cookie cutter. Printers often keep a supply of standard dies for common items such as pocket folders and table tents. Cutting labels and decals from printed paper, but not its backing, is called *kiss die cutting*. Sheets printed this way allow the label or decal to be peeled away from the backing.

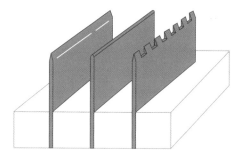

Shown, from left to right, are dies for cutting, scoring, and perforating.

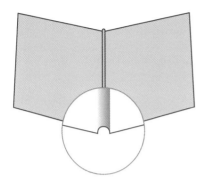

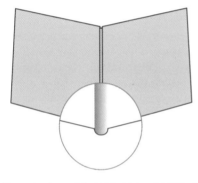

When a piece is scored, the fold should always be made with the ridge or hinge on the inside for minimum stretch.

*Scoring:* To facilitate folding, a crease is applied using the metal edge of either a rule or a wheel so that an embossed ridge on the paper is formed. Heavy text and cover stocks should always be scored. Scoring is especially important to prevent cracked ink on fold lines when using coated stocks with heavy ink coverage.

*Perforating:* Perforating involves punching a line of holes to make tearing easier. It can be done as part of the binding process to make signatures easier to fold before they are bound and trimmed as part of a publication, or as a means of facilitating tear-offs on pieces that include response vehicles, such as business reply cards.

*Drilling/punching:* Pieces that are ring or post bound require holes ranging between $1/8"$ and $1/4"$. Commercial printers and binderies use a drill to make these holes according to size and placement specifications. Spiral and plastic comb binding require punching holes, a process that costs a bit more than drilling.

## Offset Inks

Most purchasers of printed products don't give ink a second thought beyond specifying a color. Although it's a good practice to let your printer choose an ink that's appropriate for the paper (or other substrate) and function of the piece, it's worthwhile to know how some inks perform as compared to others.

*High gloss:* Ink formulation includes a high content of varnish for maximum sheen. Most effective when used on coated and cast-coated stocks. Not appropriate for heat drying, which can reduce gloss.

*Heat set:* Quick-drying inks used in web offset. Ink solvents are vaporized as they pass through a heating chamber at the end of the press. The ink is then set as it passes through cooling rolls.

*Metallic:* Made from a mixture of metal dust and varnish, metallic inks have the greatest effect on coated paper. They have a tendency to rub off if the ink has been laid down thickly. Some metallics, such as copper, can also have a tendency to tarnish. An overlay of varnish can minimize these problems.

*Fluorescent:* More opaque and vibrant than standard inks, fluorescents can also be mixed with process inks to increase their vibrancy. Fluorescents don't always retain their colorfastness as long as standard inks and may not be suitable for pieces with a long shelf life or those that will be exposed to sunlight.

*Soy based:* Inks made with a high content of soy bean oil rather than petroleum. Soy-based inks don't release volatile organic compounds that cause air pollution when they dry. They offer saturated color and solid coverage, but are generally more expensive and may require longer drying time than standard inks.

## Varnishes and Protective Liquid Coatings

Varnishes and other liquid coatings are applied to protect the inked surface of a piece or to enhance a design, either by dulling or applying a glossy finish to the surface. A range of protection and aesthetic possibilities exists, with each type of coating offering its own set of advantages. As a general rule, varnishes and liquid coatings work best on coated papers. They tend to be absorbed into uncoated papers, creating a mottled appearance.

Coatings also need to be compatible with the type of ink used. Metallics, and other pigments as well as other ingredients in the ink may present a problem. Be sure to let your printer know what type of coating or laminate will be used to ensure that a compatible ink is used for the project.

*Spot varnish:* A clear coating is applied on press or in line, just as another ink would be to isolated areas on a piece. Spot varnish costs no more than another ink color would cost. Spot varnish comes in glossy or dull finishes and can also be lightly tinted with other inks. Spot gloss varnish is often used to enhance photographs and other imagery by giving them a high sheen and richness similar to the effect achieved with the high-gloss paper used for photographic prints. In contrast, dull varnish is often applied only to areas of text on a glossy, coated paper to prevent glare and make photographs and other imagery stand out. It offers little protection against scuffing, dirt and spills, but some protection against fingerprints. Spot varnish can also prevent flaking and rub-off when applied to metallic inks.

*Aqueous coating:* A glossy coating made from a mix of polymers and water that is often applied to magazine and brochure covers as a means of protection against scuffing, dirt, and water. Aqueous coatings are applied as a flood varnish, meaning that the entire sheet is covered, at the end of the pressrun. Aqueous coatings require a special coating unit that is usually installed at the end of the press, and they cost about twice as much as a spot varnish.

*Ultraviolet or UV coating:* An ultraviolet light-cured process that involves a plastic liquid, ultraviolet coatings offers more protection and a higher degree of gloss than aqueous coating. Some printers can apply ultraviolet coating in line, but it is most often applied as a separate operation, often by screen printing as either a flood or spot varnish or applied with a roller unit as a flood varnish. The roller-applied process is more economical for long runs, whereas, screen printing is more cost-effective for short runs. When applying UV coatings, use wax-free inks. Although UV coating is available in a dull finish, it is more expensive than gloss. The durable finish of ultraviolet coating is most often used on pocket folders, book covers and table tents. Because its hard plastic surface may crack at fold lines, care should be taken when scoring and folding UV-coated pieces.

## GLOSSY VERSUS MATTE FINISHES

When deciding whether to use a glossy versus a dull or matte coating or laminate, take into consideration the piece's function and whether or not additional pressruns may be involved:

• Matte or dull coatings or laminates on white paper tend to show dirt more than glossy laminates and coatings.

• Glossy coatings and laminates are more likely to show fingerprints than those with a dull or matte finish.

• Glossy coatings and laminates are more likely to present a problem if inkjet printing (such as addressing) is planned as part of the finishing process. This often requires inkjet printed labels instead. However, recent advances in inkjet technology have made some printers capable of inkjet printing on a glossy surface. Check with your printer and mail house to determine the best course of action.

## Laminates

Laminating offers the best protection of all methods, yielding an exceptionally strong surface that repels moisture that can even be washed. The process involves adhering a layer of polyester, polypropylene, or nylon film to one or both sides of the printed sheet. Laminates are available in thicknesses from 0.001 inch (0.0251 mm) to 0.010 inch (0.251 mm) in both gloss and dull finishes, as well as a satin finish that falls in between. Thinner films are more appropriate for book covers and packaging, whereas, thicker films are better suited for menus, displays, and name tags. Laminating costs more than varnishes and liquid coatings, with the exception of UV matte.

When selecting the most appropriate laminate for a project, keep the following considerations in mind:

*Nylon laminates:* These durable laminates are the most expensive, but their porosity helps prevent paper curl by allowing gasses and moisture to leave the underlying paper. Nylon laminates are recommended for lightweight substrates such as paperback covers, and applications where metallic inks are involved.

*Polyester laminates:* Their hard surface and median price makes polyester laminates appropriate for case-bound books and situations where durability and longevity are important.

*Polypropylene laminates:* Laminates made of this material are often used on dust jackets and packaging. Although they are softer than other laminates and more likely to be scuffed and scratched, polypropylene laminates are the least expensive. Polypropylene laminates can also be applied to lightweight substrates and surfaces printed with metallic inks without fear of curling.

## PROOFING METHODS

Proofs help designers and others know, before beginning press production, how a piece will look and feel when it has been printed and assembled. They also serve as a means of checking how a digital file will print, and to ensure that type, imagery, and color will print as specified.

A broad range of proofing possibilities exists. Which method you choose depends largely on what aspect of a job is being checked. In many cases, one type of proof will be adequate in the early stages of a job, whereas, others will be more useful as the job progresses.

*Paper dummy:* A paper dummy is a non-printed sample assembled to project specifications with the paper that has been specified for the job. Although paper dummies do not show how a job will look when printed, they are useful for showing how bulky a document will be and how much it will weigh, if mailing costs are a consideration. Paper dummies are useful when making paper choices for pocket folders, direct mail pieces, and all other types of publications.

*Ink drawdowns:* Provided by the ink supplier to the printer, ink drawdowns are used for determining how the ink and paper will interact before going on press. Generally prepared in 12 × 6" (304.8 × 152.4 mm) strips, drawdowns are often used to determine absorption rates on uncoated papers and for matching critical colors, such as a corporate colors, on different types of papers.

*Bluelines:* Photosensitive paper is combined and exposed with film negatives for a job to give a one-color (blue) representation of how the job will print. Bluelines work well for checking the placement of text and images, cropping and image size as well as crossovers, folds, and page sequencing. They are not suitable for checking color or image quality. They can only be generated when film negatives are produced as part of the job. Also called *Dyluxes.*

*Analog color proofs:* Analog color proofs involve overlays, made directly from film negatives that record each color on a separate sheet of clear polyester film. The films are taped or laminated together in register to give a representation much like a color print. Dyes for these proofs are matched to inks to simulate the finished, printed piece. Because they are made from the negatives that will print the final job, analog proofs have long been regarded as the most accurate means of determining imaging and color accuracy. Cromalin and Color Key are both brand names for this type of proofing system.

*Digital proofs:* Digital proofs range from simple black-and-white laser prints, generated from a studio printer, to sophisticated color proofs that simulate how a job will look when it is finally produced on press. Digital proofs are your only option if offset plates are generated directly from digital files without producing negatives—an option commercial printers are increasingly turning to as digital prepress technology becomes more sophisticated and color accuracy more reliable. Processes include prints generated by laser, thermal, dye sublimation, or ink-jet printers.

# Glossary

## A

**A sheets:** ISO paper sizes based on metric dimensions. The ISO standard is used everywhere except North America for determining standard trim sizes.

**Accordion fold:** Zigzag type of fold in a sheet of paper where two or more parallel folds open in the manner of an accordion, permitting the paper to be extended to its full breadth with a single pull. Also called a *fan fold*.

**Aqueous coating:** A water-based coating that is applied at the end of a press run to protect a printed piece against moisture, dirt, and scuffing.

## B

**B sheets:** ISO paper sizes slightly larger than A sheets. The ISO standard is used everywhere except North America for determining standard trim sizes.

**Bar code:** A series of horizontal or vertical parallel lines representing a code that can be optically read and interpreted by a bar code scanner.

**Barrel fold:** Fold style where the outer edge of each panel or page is folded in toward the other resulting in six panels or pages. Also called roll fold.

**Basis weight:** In the U.S. and Canada, the weight, in pounds, of a ream (five hundred sheets) of paper cut to basic size.

**Bitmap:** Computer image comprised of pixels.

**Blanket:** Rubber-coated pad mounted on a cylinder of an offset press that receives the inked image from the plate and transfers it to the paper surface.

**Bleed:** A printed area that extends beyond the trimmed edge of a printed piece. Bleed areas generally range from 1/8" to 1/4" (3.175 mm to 6.35 mm).

Bleeds are produced by printing a piece on a sheet of paper larger than the trim size of the final piece and then cutting away the edges.

**Blister pack:** Packaging mounted on a card and encased under a plastic dome.

**Blueline:** A photographic contact print made from plate-ready negatives used as a proof to show positioning of images, cropping, and page sequence. Also called a Dylux or brownline.

**Board paper:** See paperboard.

**Body copy:** See text.

**Boldface:** Type that is darker and heavier than the rest of the text with which it is used.

**Bond:** Grade of paper used for photocopying, envelopes, office correspondence, and flyers.

**Brightness:** The amount of light reflectivity a given paper has.

**Bristol:** General term for stock 6 points or thicker with a basis weight between 90# and 200# (200–500 gsm). Used for index cards, file folders, and postcards.

**Brownline:** See blueline.

**Bulking dummy:** A dummy assembled from the paper specified for a printing job.

**Butt:** To join two elements edge to edge.

## C

**C sizes:** ISO paper sizes with correct dimensions for folders and envelopes for items trimmed to A sizes.

**Camera ready:** Term describing an image or layout that is ready for print reproduction.

**Case bind:** Binding that uses glue to hold signatures to a case made of binder board covered with plastic, fabric, or leather.

**Caption:** A word, phrase, or sentence that is placed in close proximity to a photograph, illustration, or other image as a means of clarifying, describing, or identifying it. Also called a *cutline*.

**Cast-coated paper:** Coated paper with a high-gloss finish achieved by pressing the paper against a metal drum while the clay coating is still wet.

**Character:** All items on the keyboard, including alphabet letters, numbers, and punctuation.

**Chipboard:** Solid cardboard used in packaging and for industrial purposes.

**Choke:** Slightly reducing an image to create a trap.

**Cromalin:** Color proofing system made from layered colored films exposed from the job's negatives.

**CMYK:** Stands for cyan, magenta, yellow, and key (black). The primary ink colors that are combined on press or as printed digital output to produce a full range of colors.

**Coarse screen:** Halftone screen that is less than 100 lpi. Most commonly used for printing on newspaper, fabric, and other rough or highly absorbent surfaces.

**Coated paper:** Paper with a smooth and sometimes glossy finish created by applying a clay coating to the surface.

**Collateral:** Ancillary print material used to support an advertising campaign.

**Color bars:** Strip of colors printed on the edge of four-color process proofs and press sheets to check registration of all colors and to evaluate ink density.

**Color break:** Where one color stops and another begins.

**Color key:** Color proofing system made from layered colored films exposed from the job's negatives.

**Column:** Blocks of type set at the same width.

**Comb binding:** Binding a publication by inserting the teeth of a flexible plastic comb through holes in a stack of paper.

**Condensed type:** Type that is narrower than surrounding text.

**Continuous-tone image:** A photograph or illustration with a range of shades not made up of halftone dots.

**Converter:** A business that does finishing work on a printed piece, such as making boxes, bags, or envelopes.

**Cover stock:** Fine printing paper with a basis weight or grammage that is heavier than text or book weight papers.

**Creep:** Where the middle pages of a folded signature extend slightly beyond the outside pages. Also called *push out* or *thrust*.

**Crop:** Trimming part of a photograph or illustration so that undesirable or unnecessary elements are eliminated.

**Crop marks:** Marks placed on the edges of a mechanical to indicate where a printed piece should be trimmed. Also called *trim marks*.

Crop marks are located outside of the final image area and indicate where a piece should be trimmed.

**Crossovers:** Where a printed area that appears on two-page spread crosses over the gutter. Also called *gutter bleed*.

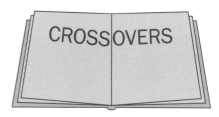

Care must be taken when printing and binding a publication to ensure that crossovers match up on two-page spreads.

**Cutline:** See caption.

## D

**Deboss:** To produce a recessed impression on the surface of a paper by pressing it between two dies.

**Deckle edge:** The edge of paper left ragged as it comes from the papermaking machine.

**Density:** The thickness of a layer of ink.

**Descender:** The part of a lowercase letter that extends below its baseline as in the letters g, j, p, and y.

**Die:** Sharp metal rules mounted on a board for making die cuts, or a solid metal block used for stamping foil or an impression on paper.

**Die-cut:** A decorative or unusual cut made in paper with a metal die.

**Display type:** Type that is larger than text type and used to grab attention. Display type usually conveys a mood or feeling and is not intended to be read in a large body of text.

**Direct mail:** Form of advertising that uses person-to-person communication by contacting individuals through the postal system.

**Dot gain:** When halftone dots print larger on paper than they are on films or plates, they reduce detail and lower contrast. Uncoated papers tend to cause more dot gain than coated papers. Also called *dot spread* or *press gain*.

**Dpi (dots per inch):** Used to measure the resolution of a scanned image. Higher dpi produces higher resolution and more detail.

**Drawdown:** Ink samples specified for a job and applied to the paper specified for the job.

**Dry mount:** Mounting art or other display materials on a rigid board using heat and pressure rather than wet adhesive.

**Dry trapping:** Printing an ink or varnish over another layer of ink or varnish after the first layer has dried.

**Dull finish:** Flat finish on coated paper

**Duotone:** Halftone made of two colors.

**Dylux:** See blueline.

## E

**Emboss:** To produce a raised impression on the surface of paper by pressing it between two dies.

**Engraving:** Printing method using a metal plate with an image cut into its surface.

**EPS (Encapsulated PostScript):** Computer file format used for placing images or graphics in documents.

**Etched plate:** Metal plate that has been etched so that its surface can be used for printing.

**Extended typeface:** Type that is wider than surrounding text.

# F

**Fan fold:** See accordion fold.

**Felt side:** Side of the paper exposed to the felt blanket during the papermaking process. The felt side is considered to be the smoothest side of the paper.

**Fifth color:** A spot or match color added on press to a four-color print run.

**FIM (facing identification mark):** A machine-detectable series of vertical bars printed in the upper corner of a business reply card or envelope that allows the US Postal System to automatically cancel letter mail.

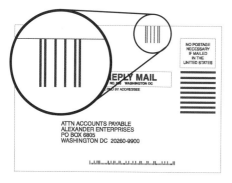

FIMs allow the US Postal Service to automatically cancel business reply cards and letters.

**Fine screen:** Halftone screen that is 100 lpi or higher. Commonly used for printing on fine printing papers with a smooth, relatively nonabsorbent surface.

**Finish:** Surface characteristics of paper. Examples of finishes include laid, linen, and vellum.

**Flexography:** Method of printing on a web press with rubber or soft plastic plates.

**Flier:** Advertising medium that is usually a single 8 1/2 × 11" (215.9 × 279.4 mm) page.

**Flood:** To print a sheet completely with an ink or varnish.

**Flush:** A term indicating that type shouldn't be indented but should be set vertically, aligned with the margin.

**Foil stamp:** Where foil and a heated die is stamped onto paper to form a printed impression.

**Folio:** The page number and other copy in the lower portion of a page, typically a title or issue date if it's a periodical.

**Font:** Equipment or software that lets a printing device print a specific typeface of type family.

**Form:** See signature.

**Four color process:** Method of printing that uses cyan, magenta, yellow, and black to reproduce full-color images. (See CMYK.)

**FPO:** Stands for "For Position Only." FPOs are stand-in replicas of imagery that will be printed. They are typically low-resolution (low-res) versions of high-resolution (high-res) images that are temporarily placed in a digital document to show how an image should be sized and cropped. When the job is printed, the low-res images are replaced with their high-res counterparts.

**French fold:** Multiple fold where the paper is first folded in half in one direction, then folded in half again, perpendicular to the first fold.

# G

**Ganging:** A cost-saving technique where a number of different items are reproduced at the same time, as in ganging several items on the same sheet of paper or separating several items at the same percentage.

**Gathered signatures:** Signatures assembled next to each other in the binding process.

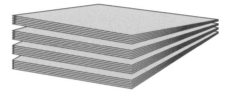

Gathered signatures are bound side by side.

**Gate fold:** A folding style where the outer edges fold inward to meet in the gutter, and then folded again at the point where they meet to form eight panels or pages.

**GIF or .gif (Graphics Interchange Format):** An 8-bit, low-memory option for posting images online.

**Grade:** A term used to distinguish between various qualities of printing papers. Examples of grades include premium and grades 1 through 5 for coated papers.

**Grammage:** The European and Asian method of measuring paper weight by representing the gram weight of one square meter of paper, expressed as grams per square meter or gsm.

**Graphic arts:** The trades, industries, and professions related to designing and printing on paper and other substrates.

**Gravure:** Printing process where the matter to be printed is etched into the printing surface. Also called *intaglio*.

**Grayscale image:** A continuous-tone black-and-white image such as a photograph or illustration.

**Grid:** The invisible framework on which a page is designed.

**Gripper edge:** The leading edge of a sheet of paper clamped by metal grippers as it is pulled through the printing press, typically about 3/8" (9.525 mm). Also called the *gripper margin*.

**Grippers:** The press mechanism that draws the paper through the cylinders of the press.

**Gutter:** The white space between columns of type or between pages on a two-page spread.

**Gutter bleed:** See crossover.

## H

**Hairline:** Minute amount of space used to describe a thin rule or close register.

**Halftone:** Reproducing a continuous tone image by photographing it through a fine screen to convert the image into a series of dots.

**Halftone dot:** Units in a halftone that, by their various sizes, re-create a continuous tone image.

A halftone screen allows a continuous tone image to printed by converting it into a series of dots.

**Haze:** See scum.

**Headline:** A sentence, phrase, word, or group of words set in large, bold type above the text on a page.

**Hickey:** A spot or imperfection on a printed piece that occurs during the print run because of a speck of dust or other particle on the press interfered with the ink's application on paper.

**High-res:** A digital image with a resolution of 200 dpi or more.

**Holdout:** See ink holdout.

**Holography:** Producing the appearance of a three-dimensional image by using a laser to overlay embossed images onto film and then onto paper.

**Hue:** A specific color.

## I

**Image:** Visual counterpart or likeness of an object, person, or a scene produced as an illustration or photograph.

**Imagesetter:** A device for outputting proofs and similar printed images or printing plates but not intended for printing multiple copies.

**Imposition:** An arrangement of pages on a printed sheet that enables them to be in the correct order when the sheet is folded and trimmed.

**Impressions per hour (iph):** A means of measuring the speed of a press.

**Imprint:** To print new copy on a previously printed sheet.

**Indicia:** Recognized by the US postal system as a means of showing that postage has been paid. Mailers using an indicia must have a bulk mailing permit.

```
BULK RATE
U.S. POSTAGE
PAID
CINCINNATI, OH
PERMIT NO. 0000
```

```
NONPROFIT ORG.
U.S. POSTAGE
PAID
SAN JUAN, PR
PERMIT NO. 0000
```

Indicias are printed on an envelope where a stamp would normally go to show that postage has been paid. A properly designed indicia identifies the user, their permit number, and the classification or rate code of the mailing.

**Industrial papers:** Papers produced for uses other than printing. Examples include kraft paper and chipboard.

**Ink fountain:** Printing press mechanism that stores and supplies ink to the printing plate or other image carrier. Rollers then transfer the ink from the fountain to the plate.

**Ink holdout:** Characteristic of a paper that prevents it from absorbing ink, allowing ink to dry on the paper's surface. Also called *holdout*.

**In-line:** Any operation tied to the printing process and done on press such as varnishing or folding.

**Intaglio:** See gravure.

**ISO standards:** Metric measurement system for paper sizes in Europe and Asia.

**Italic:** Type style with characters slanted upward to the right. Used to emphasize a word or passage.

## J

**Jogging:** To straighten or align the edges of a stack of paper by jostling them.

**JPEG:** File format designated by the Joint Photographic Experts Group for image compression. JPEGs are frequently used for placing imagery in websites and online applications.

## K

**Kerning:** Adjusting the amount of space between letters or characters so that letter spacing appears to be in balance.

# PLAY

Before kerning.

# PLAY

After kerning. The space has been adjusted between the letterforms so that spacing appears more balanced.

**Kiss die cut:** A process used for peel-off labels where a die cut is made through the face materials but not the backing.

**Kraft:** Strong paper made from unbleached wood pulp that is often used for paper bags and wrapping paper.

## L

**Laminate:** A means of bonding plastic film to a sheet of paper using heat and pressure.

**Leading:** The amount of vertical space between lines of type.

**Lenticular printing:** Printing process involving animated effects that flip back and forth as the viewing angle changes.

**Letterpress:** The process of printing from an inked raised surface.

**Letterspacing:** Modifying the distance between the letters in a word. Also called *tracking* or *kerning*.

# Play

Without letterspacing.

# Play

After letterspacing.

**Line art:** A black-and-white image that is not continuous tone or does not include any grays. Also called *line drawing* or *line copy*.

**Line count:** See screen ruling.

**Lithography:** The process of printing from a flat surface (such as a smooth stone or metal plate) that has been treated so that the image area is ink receptive and the nonimage area is ink repellant.

**Logo:** A unique design, symbol, or typographic treatment that represents a company or brand.

**Logotype:** A logo comprising typographic forms, usually a unique typographic treatment of a company's name.

**Low-res:** A digital image with a resolution of 100 dpi or less.

**Lpi (lines per inch):** A means of measuring the fineness of a halftone screen by measuring the number of dots per inch in a halftone screen.

## M

**Makeready:** Getting a printing press ready for a print run by filling the ink fountains, adjusting the paper feeder, etc.

**Margin:** White space at the top, bottom, and to the left and right of a body of type.

**Masthead:** The name of a newspaper, magazine, or other periodical displayed on the cover. Also used to describe the area where a periodical and its publisher's name, address, and staff credits appear.

**Match color:** Flat ink colors that are matched to swatches. Also called *spot color.*

**Matchprint:** A digital proof that uses toner to replicate the process colors. Matchprints are *close* to cromalin color accuracy but are markedly less expensive.

**Mask:** A means of isolating a portion of an image from its surrounding area so that it becomes a silhouette or outline image.

**Matte:** A flat, not glossy, finish on a paper or photograph.

**Mechanical:** A document with type, graphic elements, and imagery in position.

**Moiré:** Undesirable patterns in printed half-tones caused by improperly aligned screens.

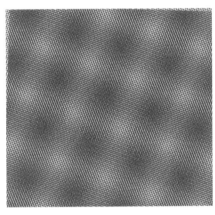

Moirés often occur when a printed halftone is screened again as it is made into a halftone.

**Mottle:** Spotty, uneven ink absorption resulting in splotchy image reproduction.

**Multicolor printing:** Printing with more than one color but fewer than four colors.

## N

**Native file format:** A file saved in the application in which it was created. Native file formats can't be transferred from one application to the next.

**Nested signature:** Where signatures are assembled inside one another before binding.

This drawing illustrates the assembly of three nested signatures prior to binding.

**Newsletter:** Information sheet or several sheets usually styled like a small newspaper.

## O

**Offset lithography:** Mostly commonly used method of printing where an image on a plate is "offset" onto a rubber blanket cylinder which, in turn, transfers the image to a sheet of paper.

**Opacity:** Characteristic of paper that prevents printing on one side from showing through on the other.

**Optical Character Recognition (OCR):** Automatic computer input process where a scanner reads printed characters and symbols and converts them to electronic data.

**Outline image:** See silhouette image.

**Overrun:** Excess production to compensate for spoilage, future requests for materials, and other unanticipated needs.

## P

**Paperboard:** Index stock over 110# and cover stock over 80# or 200 gsm commonly used in packaging. Also called *board paper*.

**PDF (Portable Document Format):** Digital file format that allows documents to be viewed and printed independent of the application used to create them.

**Perfect binding:** A method of binding magazines, books, and other publications in which the signatures are glued to the cover and held together with a strip of adhesive.

**Pica:** Unit of typographic measure equal to 0.166 inch (4.218 mm).

**PICT:** Macintosh image file format.

**Prepress:** Preparing a job for print reproduction by performing necessary functions such as separating, color correcting, and impositioning the pages.

**PMS:** Stands for Pantone Matching System, a means of specifying match or spot colors and their ink formulations.

**Point:** A typographic measurement system used for measuring the height of type, thickness of rules, and leading.

**PostScript:** Computer language that allows digital files to be printed on desktop printers and imagesetters.

**Press gain:** See dot gain.

**Pressure-sensitive label:** A label with an adhesive backing that can be peeled off, and the label applied to another surface by pressure.

**Printer font:** A font that allows a printing device to output a typeface.

**Printer's spreads:** Pages that are set up so they are impositioned exactly where they will be when a publication is folded and printed.

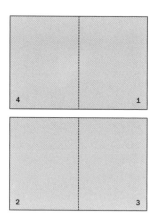

When a four-page signature is set up as printer's spreads, pages 2 and 3, and pages 1 and 4 face each other.

**Printing plate:** A surface carrying an image to be printed.

**Process color:** The inks used in four-color process printing. Ink colors consist of cyan, magenta, yellow, and black.

**Proof:** A test sheet made to represent how a final printed product will look so that flaws may be corrected before the piece is printed.

## Q

**Quadratone:** Halftone comprising four colors, usually to create a rich tonal range but not comprising the four process colors (cyan, yellow, magenta, and black).

## R

**Raster image processing (RIP):** Converting digital files to bitmapped images that can be output on an imagesetter. The rocess is described as "ripping a file."

**Reader's spreads:** Pages that are set up as they will be read (left- and right-hand pages side by side.)

**Ream:** Five hundred sheets of paper.

**Reflective art:** Photographs, illustrations, and other imagery that is scanned or viewed as an item that reflects light. Also called *reflective copy, hard copy, or reflective imagery*.

**Register:** When each sheet enters the press from precisely the same position ensuring that all colors are in "register."

**Register marks:** Targetlike symbol placed in exactly the same spot for each color plate so that proper alignment of the colors will occur on press.

Register marks help printers keep colors in alignment as a piece passes through the different ink stations on a press.

**Resolution:** The quantification of print quality using the number of dots per inch in electronic imaging.

**Reverse:** A white or noncolor image against a dark, inked, or colored background.

**RGB:** Stands for red, green, and blue, additive primary colors that are used to create a full range of color as projected light on a computer screen.

**Roll fold:** See barrel fold.

**Rule:** A line set as part of typesetting.

## S

**Saddle stitch:** A method of binding by stitching through the centerfold of nested signatures.

**Saturation:** The degree to which a color is pure and free of dilution from black, white, or gray.

**Scanner:** A device that converts images on film or paper into digital information.

**Score:** To crease or indent paper along a straight line so it folds more easily and accurately.

**Screen font:** Font that can be viewed on a computer monitor.

**Screen printing:** See silk screen.

**Screen ruling:** Number of rows or lines of dots per inch in a screen for making a screen tint or halftone. Also called *line count*, *screen frequency*, *screen size*, or *screen value*.

**Screw and post binding:** Binding that secures pages with a bolt that is inserted through a drilled hole and secured with a post on the opposite side.

**Scum:** A thin haze of ink that appears in on-image areas on a printed sheet. Also called *haze*.

**Separations:** Reproducing a color image by dividing it into four negatives, one each for cyan, magenta, yellow, and black.

**Serigraphy:** See silk screen.

**Sheetfed:** A printing process utilizing sheets of paper rather than rolls.

**Shingling:** The allowance made during page impositioning to compensate for creep. Also called *stair stepping* or *progressive margins*.

**Show through:** Areas where an image printed on one side of a sheet can be seen on the opposite side. Show through occurs when the paper is too thin for the ink application.

**Shrink-wrap:** A method of securely wrapping packages, loose items, or products in clear plastic film.

**Side stitch:** To bind by stapling through pages along one edge. Also called *side wire*.

**Signature:** A printed sheet folded at least once, possibly many times, to become part of a book, magazine, or other publication. Signatures are commonly made up of four, eight, sixteen, or thirty-two pages. Also called a *form*.

**Silk screen:** A method of printing where ink is forced through a stencil adhered to a screen. Also called *serigraphy* or *screen printing*.

**Silhouette halftone:** A halftone image from which the background has been removed, usually through masking. Also called *outline halftone*.

**Small caps:** Capital letters smaller than the capital letters in a typeface.

**Spoilage:** Paper that is recycled as a result of on-press mistakes and accidents.

**Spot color:** See match color.

**Spread:** Slightly enlarging an image to create a trap.

**Stet:** Latin for "let it stand." Proofreader's or editor's indication that an item marked for correction should remain as it was before the correction.

**Supercalendered:** Paper that has passed through metal and fiber rollers to produce a smooth, glossy finish.

**SWOP (Specifications for Web Offset Publications):** Recommended printing specifications published every few years by a committee of graphic arts professionals.

## T

**Text:** The body of written material on a page or document. Also called *body copy*.

**Text paper:** Fine printing papers with a basis weight or grammage that falls in-between cover and writing or bond weights.

**Thermography:** A method of printing where a raised impression is created by heat curing a blend of ink and resin.

**TIFF (Tagged Image File Format):** Used for placing images or graphics in documents created in word processing, page layout, or drawing programs.

**Tint:** See value.

**Tonal range:** Difference between the darkest and lightest area of a continuous tone image.

**Tonal compression:** The reduction of the tonal range in an image to facilitate image reproduction.

**Tracking:** See letterspacing.

**Trademark:** A slogan, name, or identifying symbol used to represent a company, product or brand.

**Transparency:** Photographic reproduction such as a 35 mm slide that is produced with a camera on transparent film.

**Transparent ink:** Ink that allows for blending through overlapping colors. Example: four-color process inks.

**Trap:** Printing one ink over another so there is a slight overlap of colors in order to prevent a colorless gap between adjacent colors if they are slightly off register.

**Tray:** A relatively shallow folding carton with a bottom hinged to the wide side and end walls.

**Trim marks:** See crop marks.

**Tri-tone:** A halftone made from three colors.

**Tube:** A carton in the shape of a rectangular sleeve formed from a sheet of board that is folded over and glued against its edges.

**Typeface:** Design of alphabetic letters, numerals, and symbols unified by consistent visual properties. Typeface designs are identified by name, such as Helvetica or Garamond.

**Type family:** A range of style variations based on a single typeface design.

**Type style:** Modifications in a typeface that create design variety while maintaining the visual character of the typeface. These include variations in weight (light, medium or bold), width (condensed or extended), or angle (italic or slanted versus roman or upright).

## U

**Uncoated paper:** Paper that has not been coated with clay.

**Unit cost:** The cost of one item in a print run arrived at by dividing the total cost of production by the number of pieces produced.

**Unsharp masking:** Adjusting an image digitally to make it appear as though it is in better focus.

**UV or ultraviolet coating:** Liquid applied to a sheet of paper that his heat cured with ultraviolet light, resulting in a hard, durable finish.

## V

**Value:** The lightness or darkness of a color. Darker values where black is added are called *shades*. Lighter values where white is added are called *tints* or *pastels*.

**Varnish:** Coating applied to paper to give it a dull or glossy finish or to provide protection against scuffing and fingerprints.

**VOC (volatile organic compounds):** Petroleum-based substances found in many printing inks.

## W

**Watermark:** A translucent impression made in a sheet of paper created during its manufacture.

**Web-fed:** A printing process utilizing paper fed through the press from a roll.

**Wet trapping:** Printing an ink or varnish over another layer of ink or varnish while the bottom layer is still wet.

**Widow:** A word or part of a word that is the last line of a paragraph or that ends up at the top of a page by itself.

**Wire-O binding:** A binding method that winds a circular, double-wire strip through prepunched holes in the cover and pages of a publication.

**Wire side:** In the papermaking process, the side of the paper that is formed against the wire. The wire side of paper made on a fourdrinier machine is generally rougher. For paper made on a cylinder machine, the wire side is generally smoother.

**Window envelope:** An envelope with an opening where part of the contents can be seen.

**Work and tumble:** Printing a sheet so that the same image is produced on both sides of a sheet. When the sheet is tumbled, the opposite side of the sheet is fed through the press.

**Work and turn:** Printing a sheet so that the same image is produced on both sides of a sheet. When the sheet is turned, the same side of the sheet is fed through the press.

**Writing paper:** Lightweight paper used for correspondence.

**Wrong reading:** An image that is backwards when compared to the original.

# Recommended Reading

**PACKAGING DESIGN AND PRODUCTION**

*Design Secrets: Packaging*
Fishel, Catharine
Rockport Publishers, 2003

*Design and Technology of Packaging Decoration for the Consumer Market*
Giles, Geoff A., ed
CRC Press, 2000

*Food Packaging Preservation*
M. Mathlouthi, ed.
Kluwer Academic Publishers, 1999

*Food Packaging Technology*
G. Bureau and J. L. Multon, eds.
Wiley-VCH, 1996

*Fundamentals of Packaging Technology*
Soroka, Walter
Institute of Packaging Professionals, 1998

*Handbook of Package Engineering*
Hanlon, Joseph F.
CRC Press, 1998

*Packaging Prototypes*
Denison, Edward and Cawthray, Richard
RotoVision, 1999

*Packaging Prototypes 2: Closures*
Emblem, Anne and Henry
RotoVision, 2001

*Packaging Prototypes 3: Thinking Green*
Denison, Edward and Yu Ren, Guang
RotoVision, 1999

*RF Measurements of Die and Packaging*
Wartenburg, Scott A.
Artech House, 2002

*The Marketer's Guide to Successful Package Design*
Meyers, Herbert M. and Lubliner, Murray J.
McGraw-Hill Contemporary Books, 1998

*The Packaging Designer's Book of Patterns*
Roth, Lazlo and Wybenga, George L.
John Wiley & Sons, 2000

*This End Up*
Mono Design
RotoVision, 2003

**PROOFREADING AND COPYWRITING**

*Chicago Manual of Style, 15th Edition*
University of Chicago Press Staff
University of Chicago Press, 2003

*Grammatically Correct: The Writer's Essential Guide to Punctuation, Spelling, Style, Usage and Grammar*
Stilman, Anne
Writers Digest Books, 1997

*The Associated Press Guide to Punctuation*
Cappon, Renee J. and Jack, ed.
Perseus Publishing, 2003

*The Associated Press Style Book and Libel Manual*
Associated Press
Addison-Wesley Publishing Company, 1982

*The Elements of Style*
Strunk, William Jr. and White, E. B.
Pearson Allyn & Bacon, 2000

*The Elements of Technical Writing*
Blake, Gary and Bly, Robert
Pearson Higher Education, 2000

*Writer's Handbook 2003*
Abbe, Elfreida
Writer, 2002

*Writing Skills Handbook*
Houghton Mifflin Company, 2002


## PAPER

*Paper Graphics*
Fishel, Catharine
Rockport Publishers, 1999

*Papers for Printing: How to Choose the Right Paper at the Right Price for Any Printing Job*
Beach, Mark; Ryan, Kathleen; and Russon, Ken
Coast to Coast Books, 1991

*The Power of Paper in Graphic Design*
Fishel, Catharine
Rockport Publishers, 2002


## IMAGING AND COLOR

*A Guide to Graphic Print Production*
Johansson, Kaj; Lundberg, Peter; and Ryberg, Robert.
John Wiley & Sons, 2003

*Color Index: Over 1100 Color Combinations, CMYK and RGB Formulas, for Print and Web Media*
Krause, Jim
How Design Books, 2002

*Digital Image Processing: Principles and Applications*
Baxes, Gregory A.
John Wiley & Sons, 1994

*Getting It Printed*
Beach, Mark and Kenly, Eric
North Light Books, 1999

*Graphic Designer's Digital Printing and Prepress Handbook*
Sidles, Constance
Rockport Publishers, 2001

*Graphics Master*
Lem, Dean
Dean Lem Associates, 2002

*Pantone Guide to Communicating with Color*
Eiseman, Leatrice
Grafix Press, Ltd., 2000

*PDF Printing and Workflow*
Romano, Frank J.
Prentice-Hall, 1998

*PDF Reference*
Adobe Systems
Addison-Wesley Publishing, 2001

*Pocket Guide to Digital Prepress*
Romano, Frank J.
Delmar Learning, 1995

*Pocket Guide to Digital Printing*
Cost, Frank
Delmar Learning, 1996

*Pocket Pal*
International Paper Staff
International Paper, 1998

*Print Production Essentials*
O'Connor, Kevin
Macmillan Publishing Company, 2003

*Process Color Manual: 24,000 CMYK Combinations for Design, Prepress and Printing*
Rogondino, Michael and Pat
Chronicle Books, 2000

*Production for Graphic Designers*
Pipes, Alan
Overlook Press, 2001

*Production for the Graphic Designer*
Craig, James
Watson-Gupthill Publications, 1990

*Professional Prepress, Printing and Publishing*
Romano, Frank J.
Prentice-Hall PTR, 1999

*Real World Color Management*
Fraser, Bruce
Peachpit Press, 2003

*The Complete Color Harmony*™
Sutton, Tina and Whelan, Bride M.
Rockport Publishers, 2004

*The Designer's Guide to Color Combinations*
Carbaga, Leslie
North Light Books, 2003

*The Designer's Lexicon: The Illustrated Dictionary of Design, Printing and Computer Terms*
Campbell, Allistair
Chronicle Books, 2000

*The Image Processing Handbook*
Russ, John C.
CRC Press, 2002

## COPYRIGHT AND TRADEMARK STANDARDS

*Copyright: Plain and Simple*
Besenjak, Cheryl
Career Press, 1997

*Getting Permission: How to License & Clear Copyrighted Materials Online & Off*
Stim, Richard
Delmar Learning, 2000

*The Public Domain: How to Find Copyright-Free Writings, Music, Art & More*
Fishman, Stephen
Nolo Press, 2001

## TYPOGRAPHY

*Adobe Type Reference Library*
Adobe Systems
Adobe Press 2002

*A Typographic Workbook: A Primer to
History, Techniques and Artistry*
Clair, Kate
John Wiley & Sons, 1999

*Basic Typography*
Craig, James
Watson-Gupthill Publications, 1990

*Designing Typefaces*
Earls, David
RotoVision, 2003

*Designing with Type: A Basic Course in
Tyopgraphy*
Craig, James; Bevington, William; and
Meyer, Susan E., ed.
Watson-Gupthill Publications, 1999

*Digital Color and Type*
Carter, Rob
RotoVision, 1996

*Encyclopaedia of Typefaces*
Jaspert, W. Pincus; Berry, W. Turner;
and Johnson, A. F.
Seven Dials, 2001

*Moving Type*
Woolman, Matt and Bellantoni, Jeff
RotoVision, 2000

*Precision Type Font Reference Guide*
Level, Jeff; Newman, Bruce; and Brenda
Hartley & Marks Publishers, 2000

*Stop Stealing Sheep and Find Out How
Type Works*
Spiekerman, Eric and Ginger, E. M.
Adobe Press, 2002

*The Complete Manual of Typography*
Felici, James
Adobe Press, 2002

*The Elements of Typographic Style*
Bringhurst, Robert
Harley & Marks Publishers, 1992

## GENERAL

*Dictionary of Marketing Terms*
Toffler, Betsy-Ann
Barron's Educational Series, Inc., 1994

*Graphic Designer's Guide to Pricing,
Estimating & Budgeting*
Williams, Theo Stephan
Allworth Press, 2001

*Idea Index: Graphic Effects and
Typographic Treatments*
Krause, Jim
North Light Books, 2003

*The Design & Printing Buyer's Survival
Guide*
Sparkman, Don
Allworth Press, 1995

*The Designer's Survival Manual*
Evans, Poppy
North Light Books, 2001

## ONLINE RESOURCES

www.acronymfinder.com
Allows users to find acronymns and abbreviations for common words and names.

www.centerforpublicdomain.org/
    copyright.htm
Answers questions about works that qualify as public domain.

www.dictionary.com
Site's search engine lets users look up word definitions.

www.grammarnow.com
Answers questions about proper word usage and grammar.

www.ipa.org
Website for the International Prepress Association offers SWOP requirements, useful publications and links to other resources.

www.loc.gov/copyright
Government site for registering copyrighted work with application downloads. Includes information on protecting copyrighted work.

www.neenahpaper.com
In addition to information on paper, website includes information on postal requirements.

www.nolo.com
Information on copyrights and cyperspace copyright infringement.

www.printing.org
Official website of the Printing Industries of America (PIA) offers helpful publications on preparing jobs for print.

www.swop.org
Website of the SWOP (Specifications for Web Offset Printing) includes guidelines for preparing and printing jobs for web offset printing.

www.uspto.gov
Government site offers information on how to display trademarks and service marks and their registration.

www.williamhouse.com
Dimensions and style reference guides for all kinds of envelopes. Tips on envelope printing and manufacturing custom envelopes.

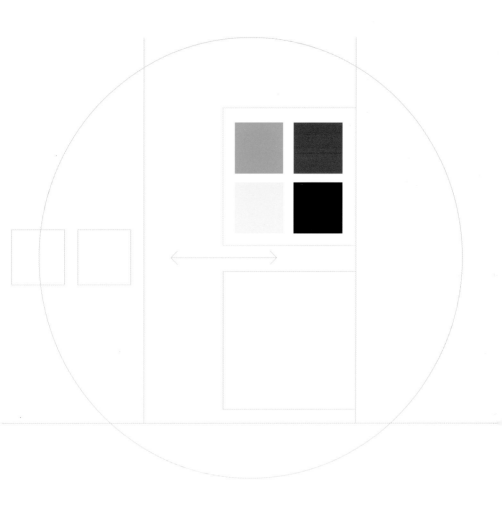

# ○ Process Color Finder

Color, when viewed on a computer screen, can look very different from a printed version of the same color. In fact, no amount of adjusting or calibrating a computer monitor can yield a truly accurate representation of how a color will look when it is printed. This difference occurs because digital color is expressed as projected light—a combination of red, green and, blue (RGB). Printed, or reflected color, is produced as a combination of cyan, yellow, magenta, and black.

The swatches in this section were created to help users visualize how a process color combination will look when it is printed. Each swatch is a percentage of one color, or a blend of a combination of percentages of the four process colors. To get accurate on-press color, find the color swatch that matches the color you would like to create on press, and then specify the screen percentage of each of the process colors that comprise that color swatch.

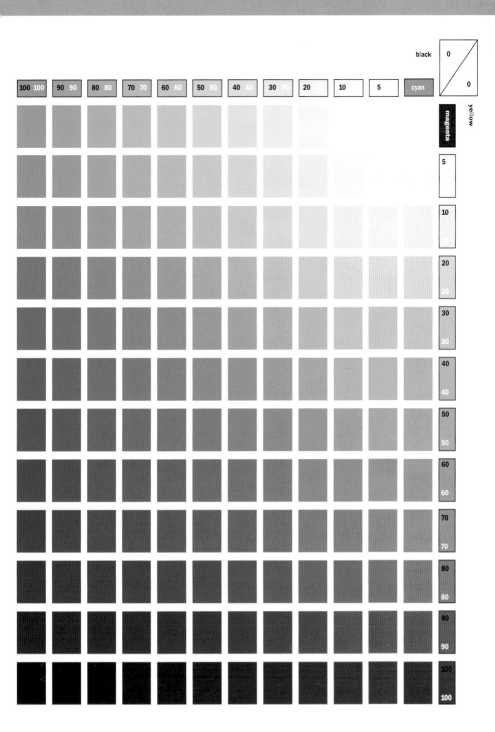

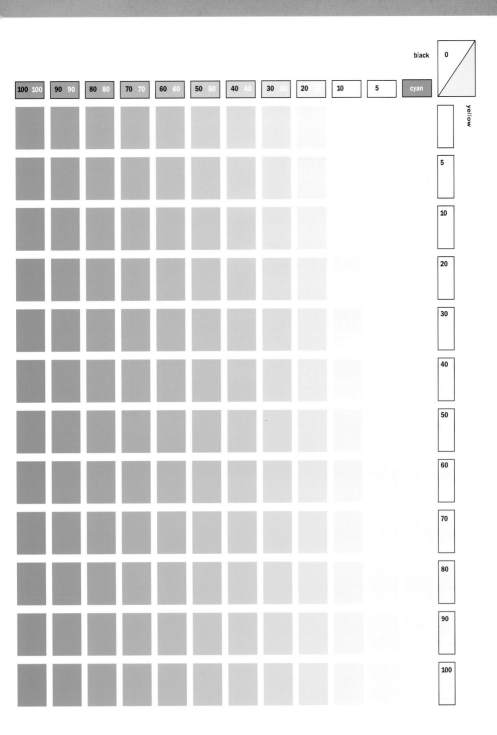

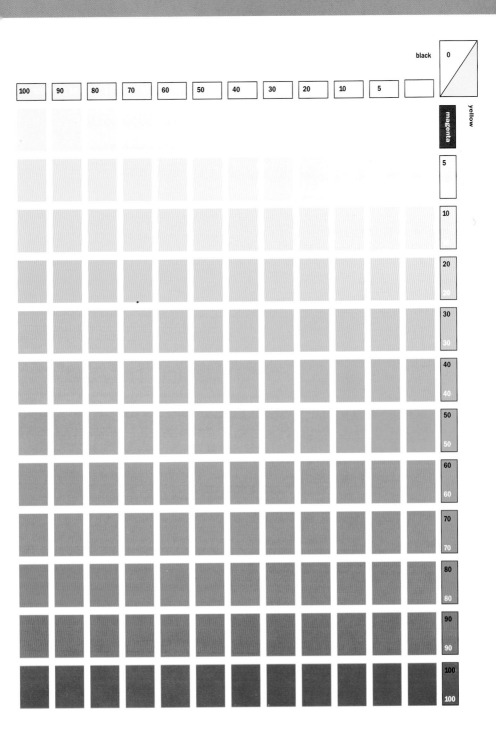

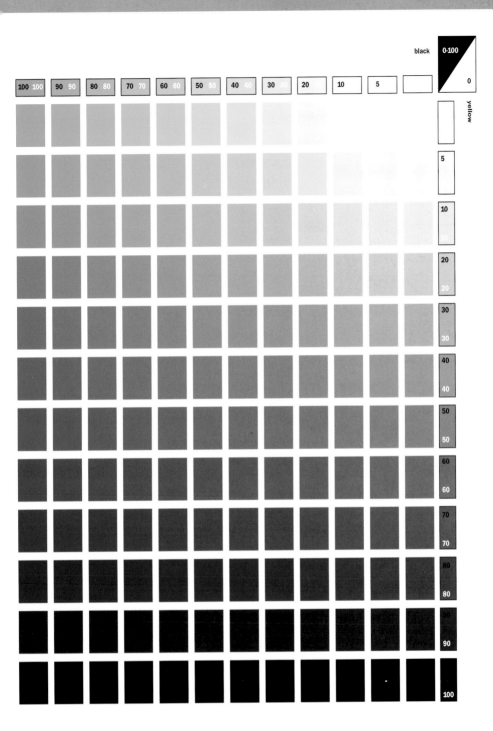

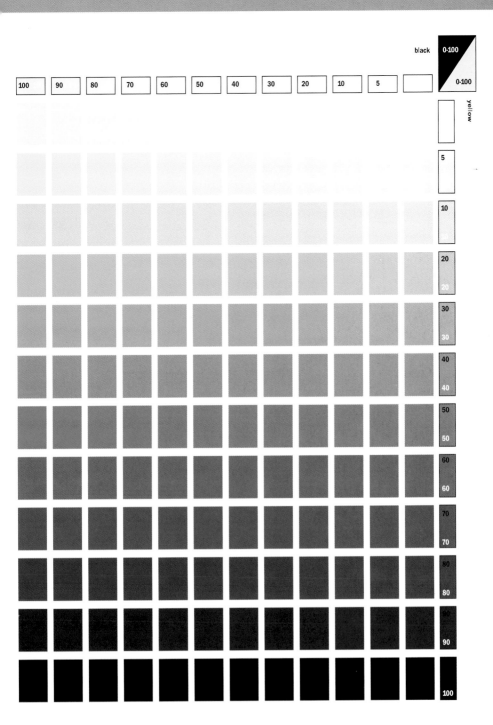

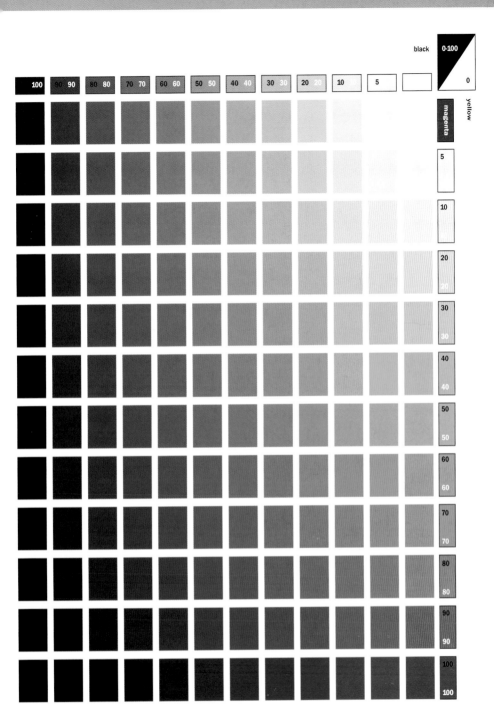

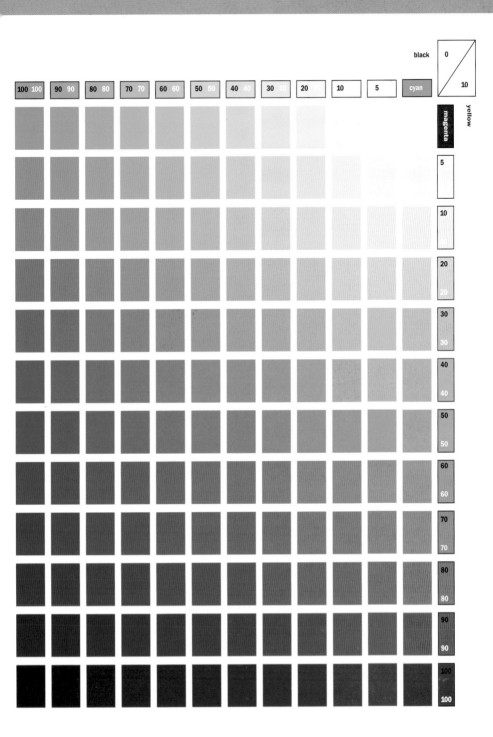

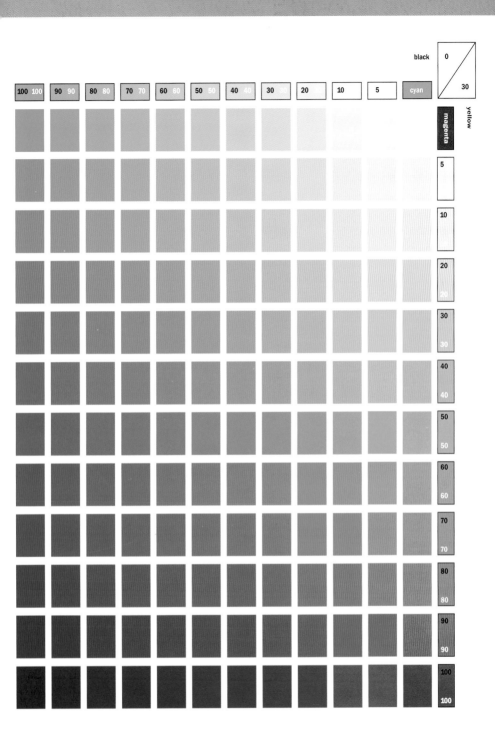

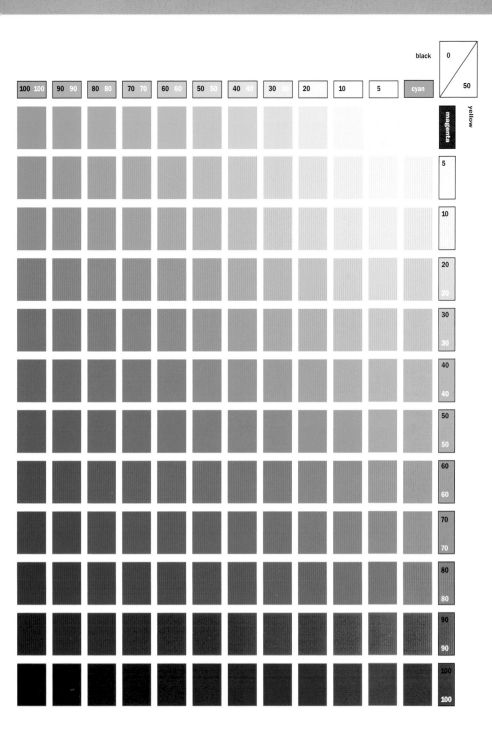

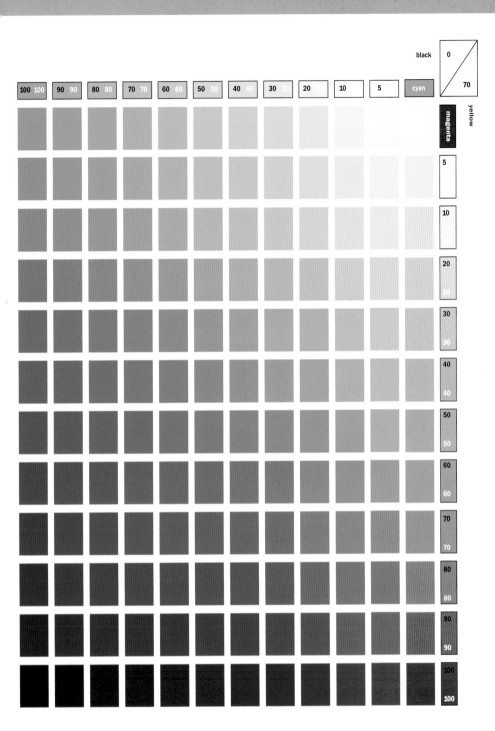

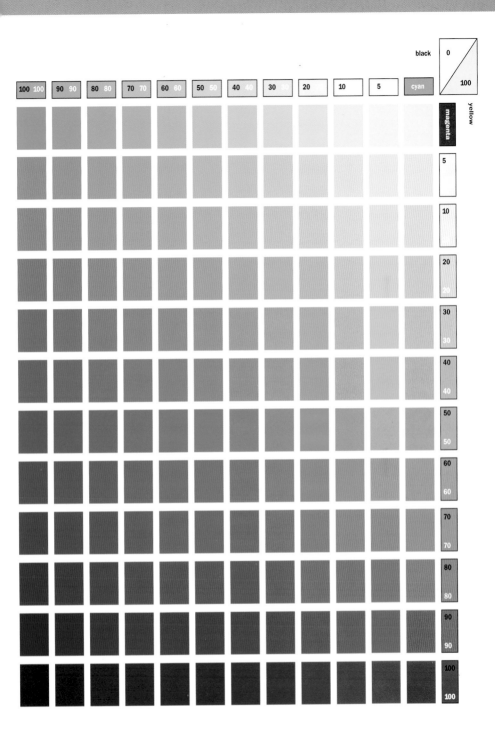

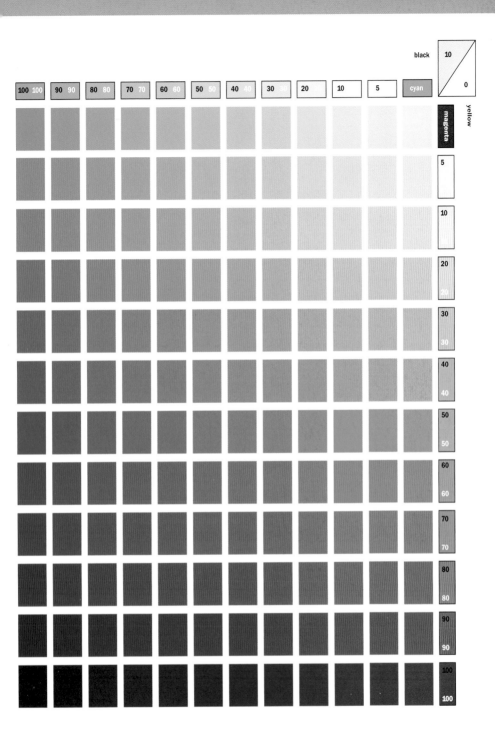

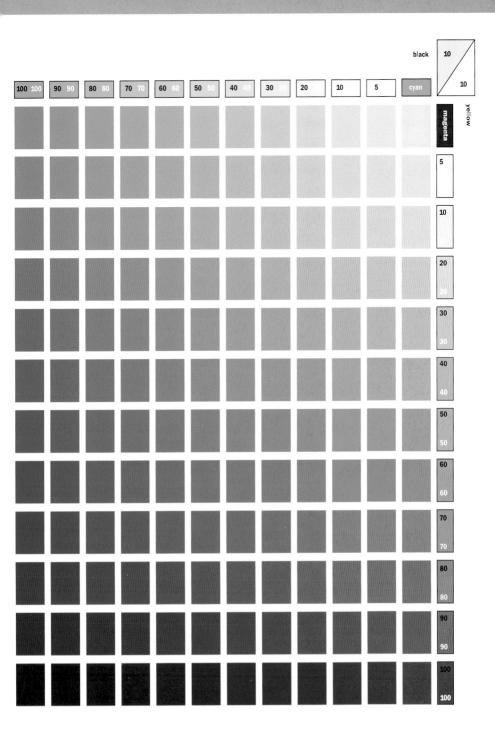

black    10

10

yellow

| 100 100 | 90 90 | 80 80 | 70 70 | 60 60 | 50 50 | 40 40 | 30 30 | 20 | 10 | 5 | cyan |
|---------|-------|-------|-------|-------|-------|-------|-------|----|----|---|------|

magenta

5

10

20

30

40

50

60

70

80

90

100

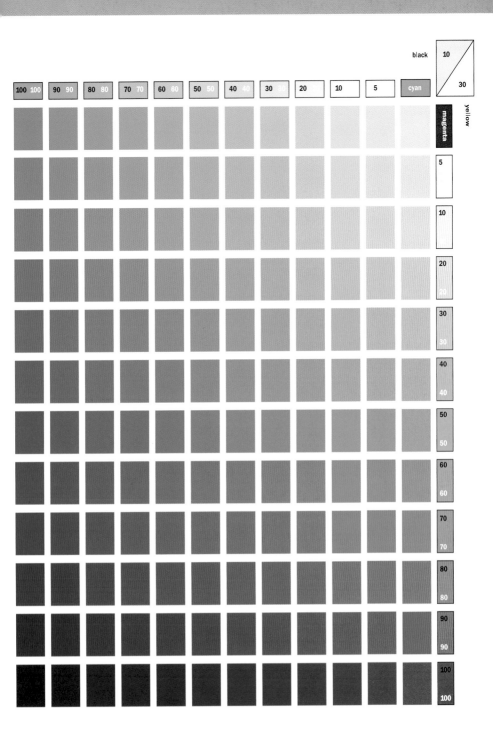

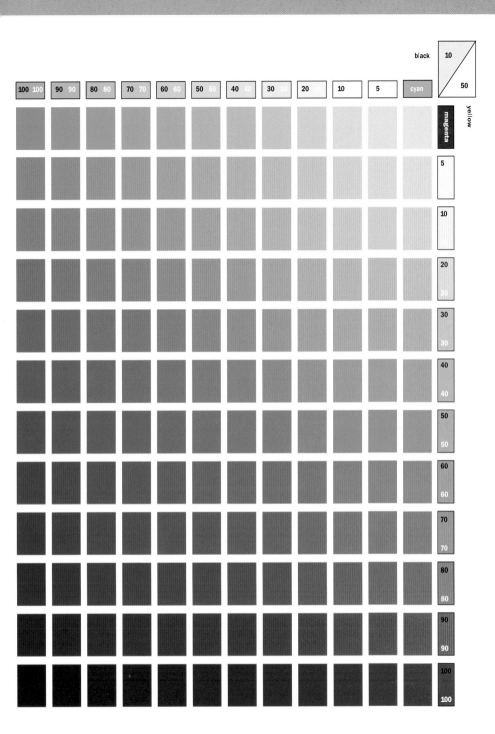

black 10

100 100 | 90 90 | 80 80 | 70 70 | 60 60 | 50 50 | 40 40 | 30 30 | 20 | 10 | 5 | cyan

50

yellow

magenta

5

10

20
20

30
30

40
40

50
50

60
60

70
70

80
80

90
90

100
100

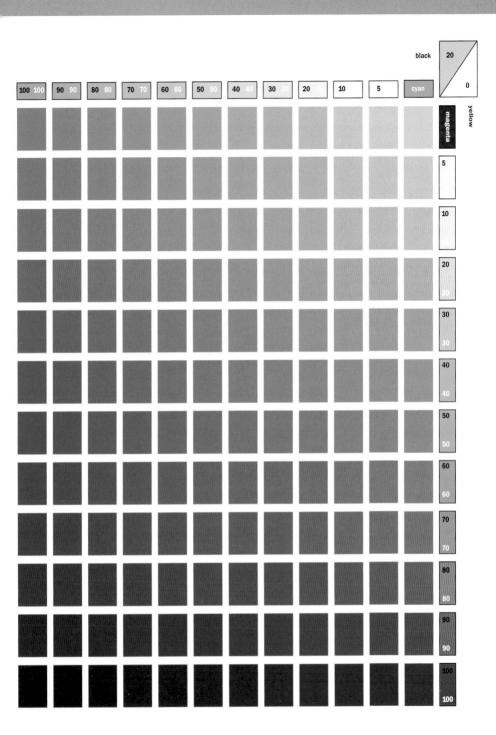

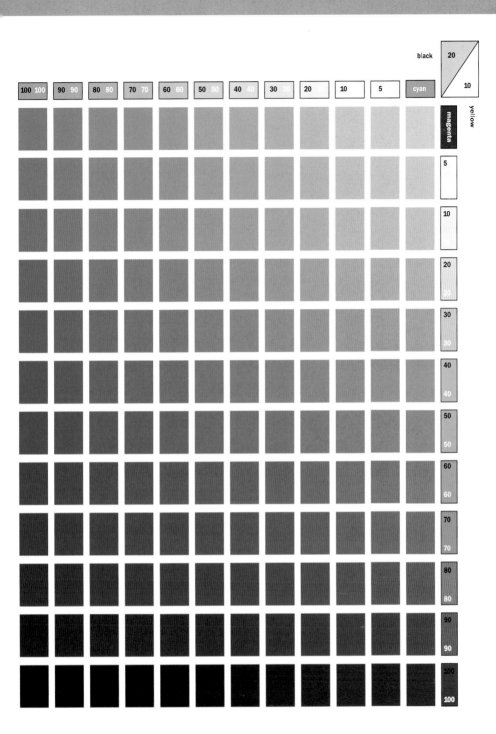

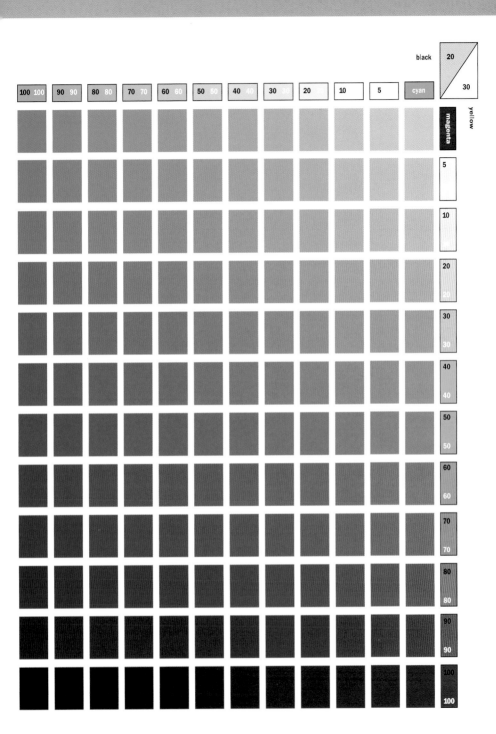

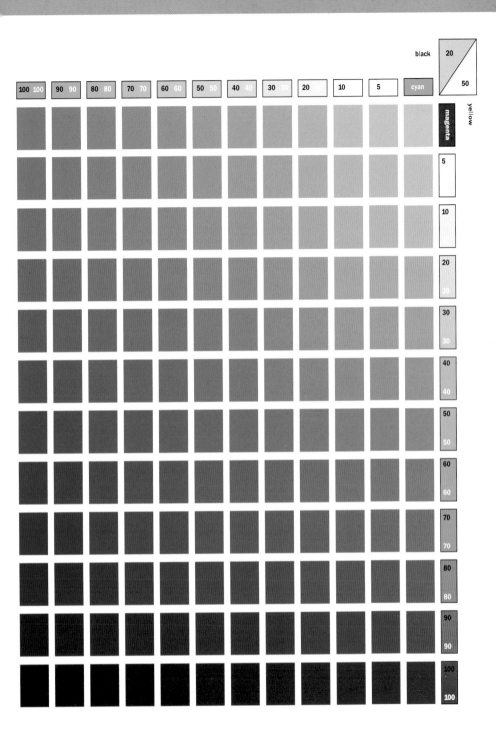

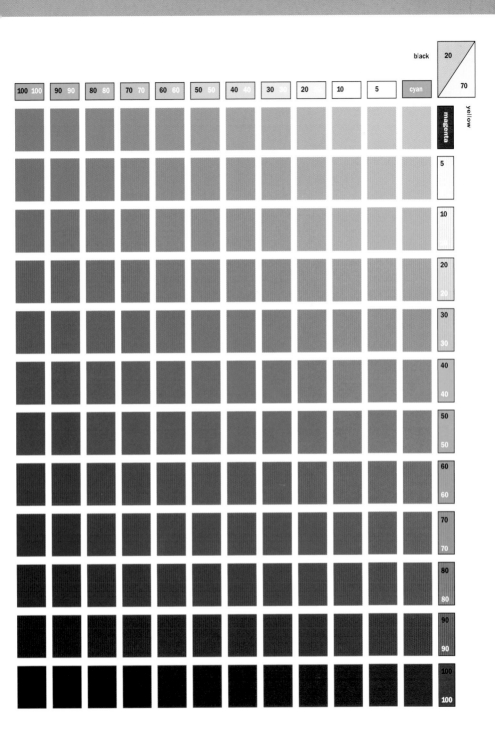

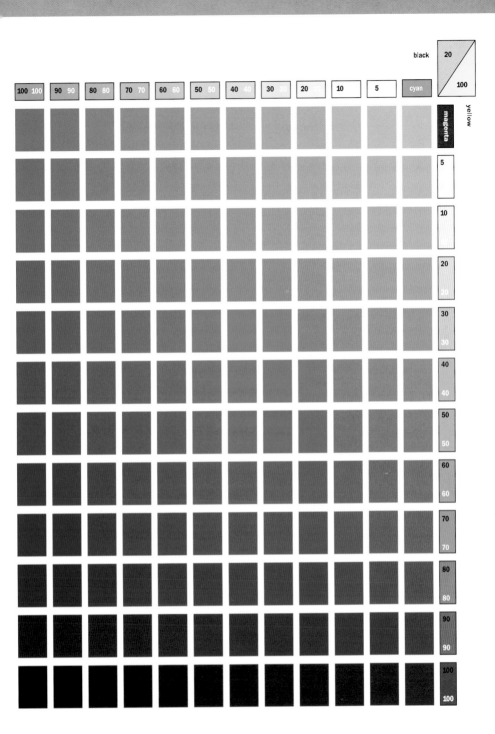

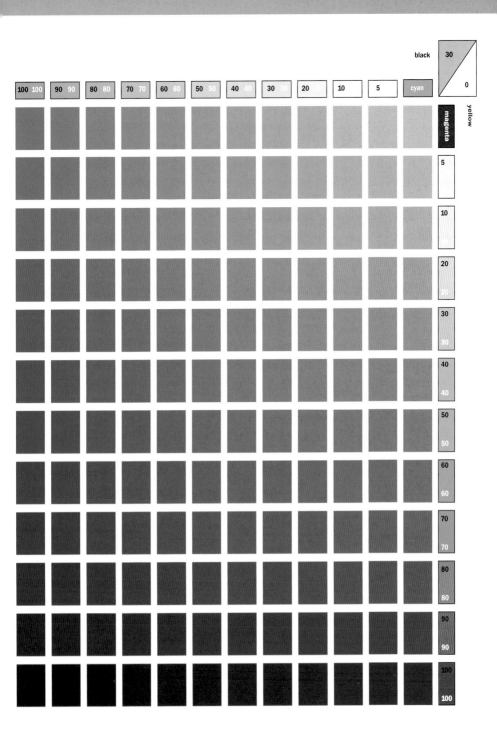

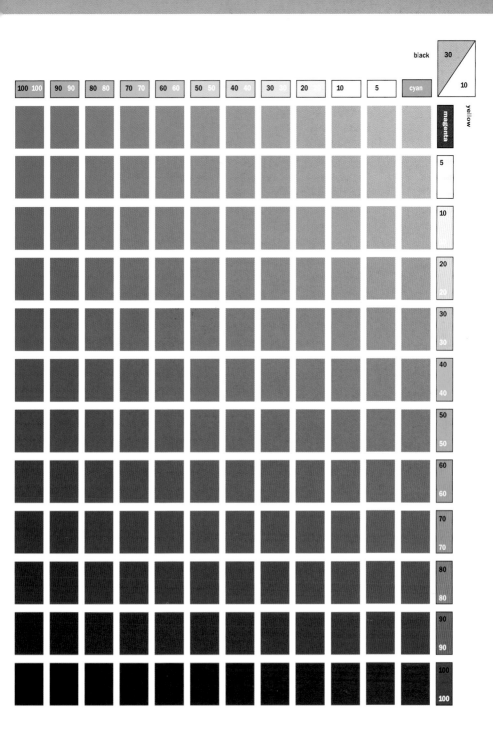

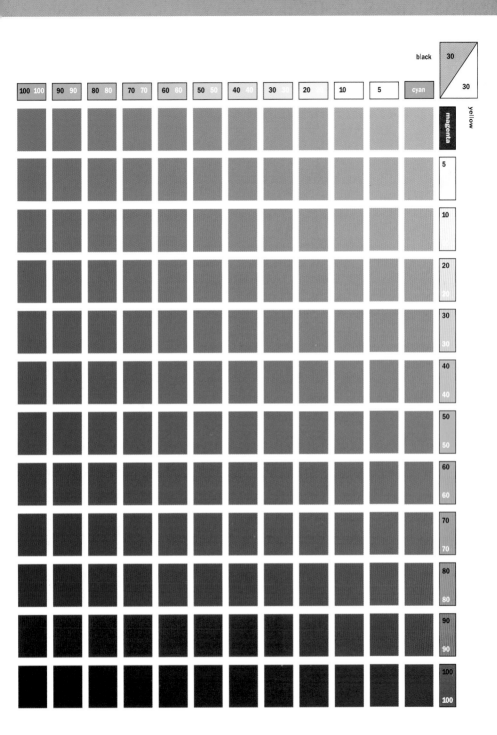

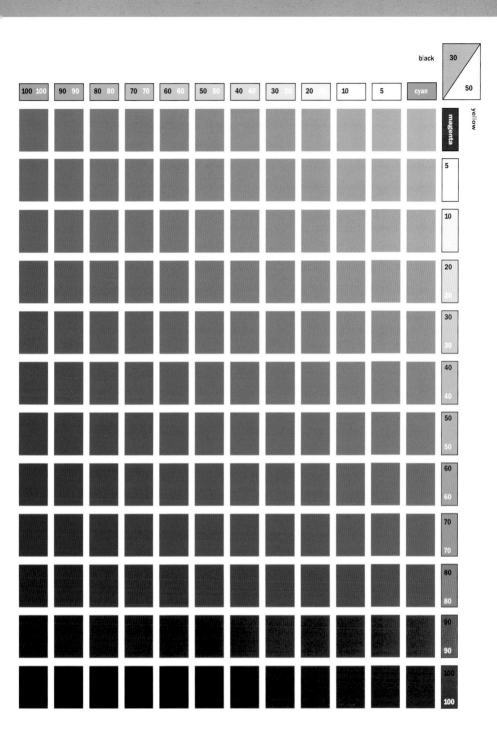

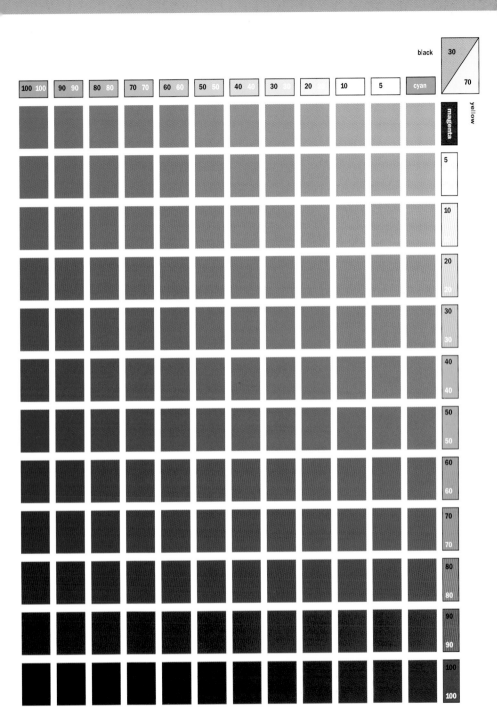

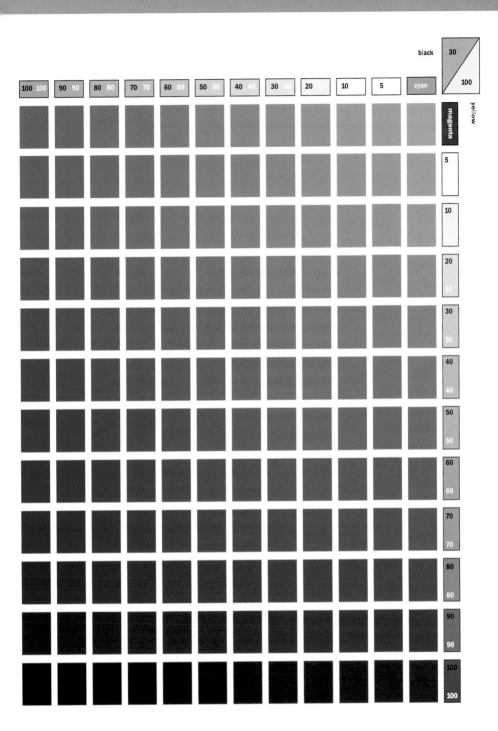

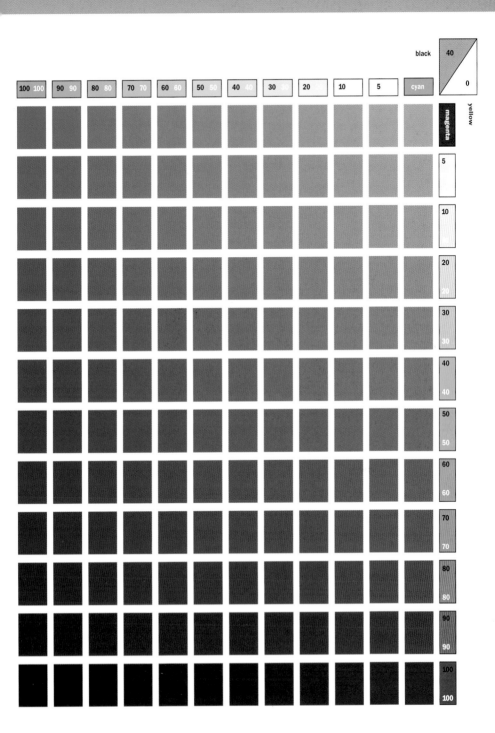

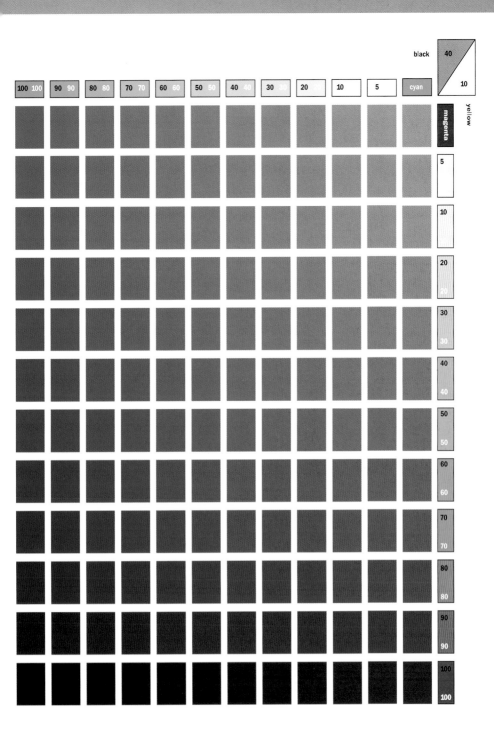

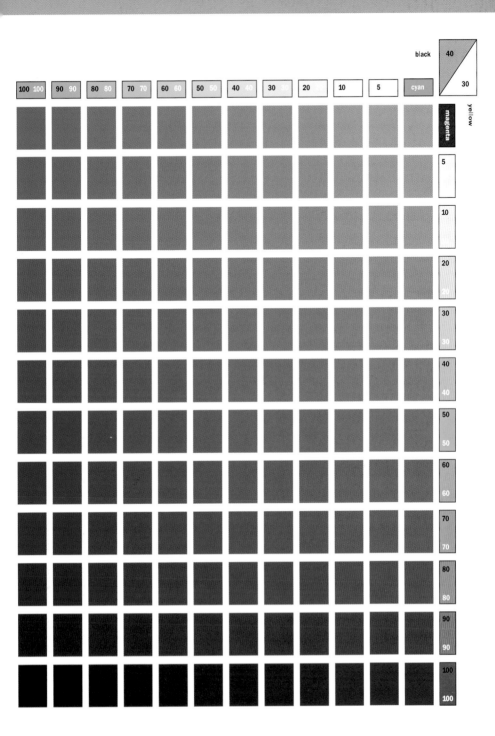

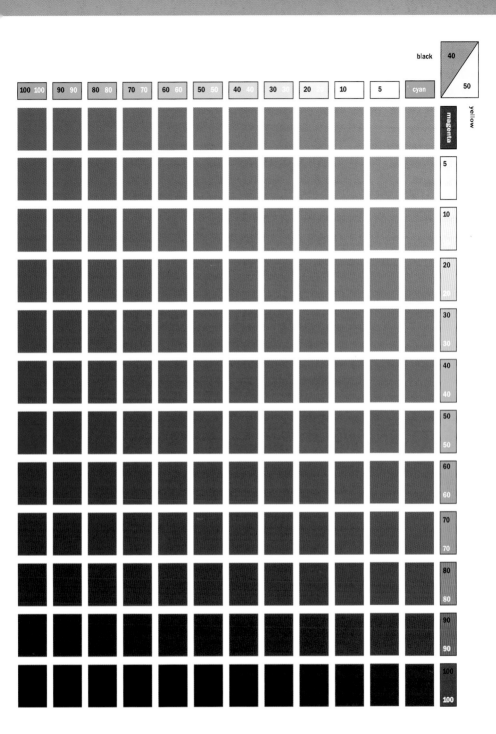

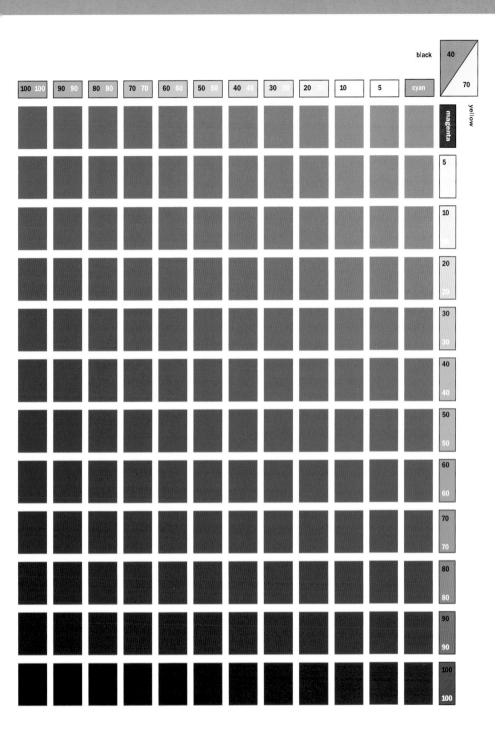

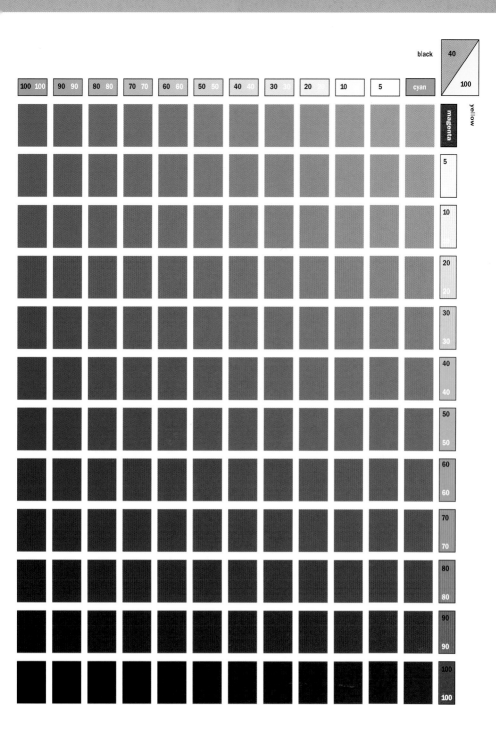

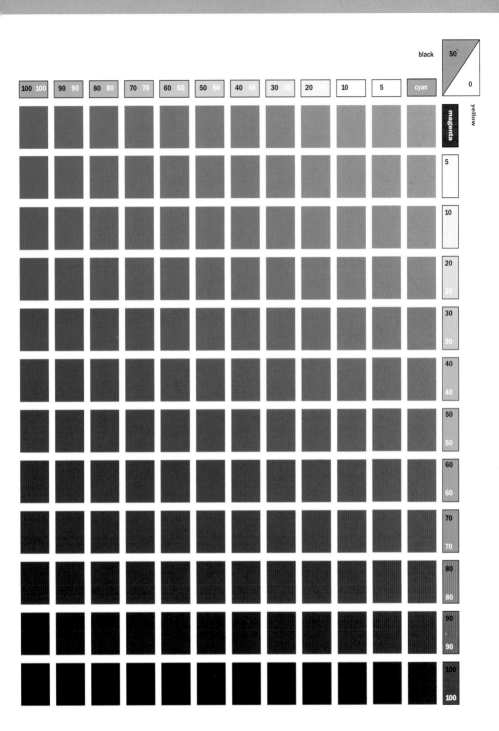

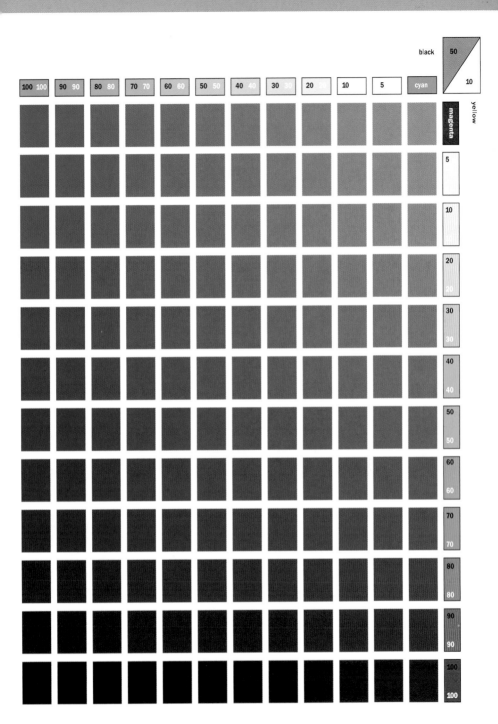

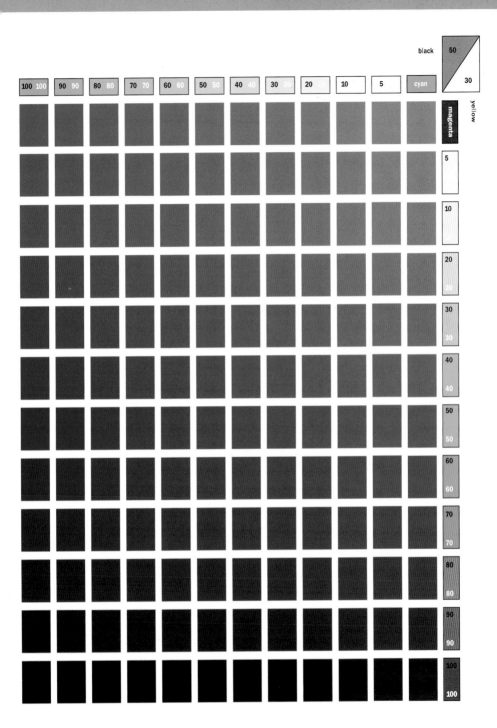

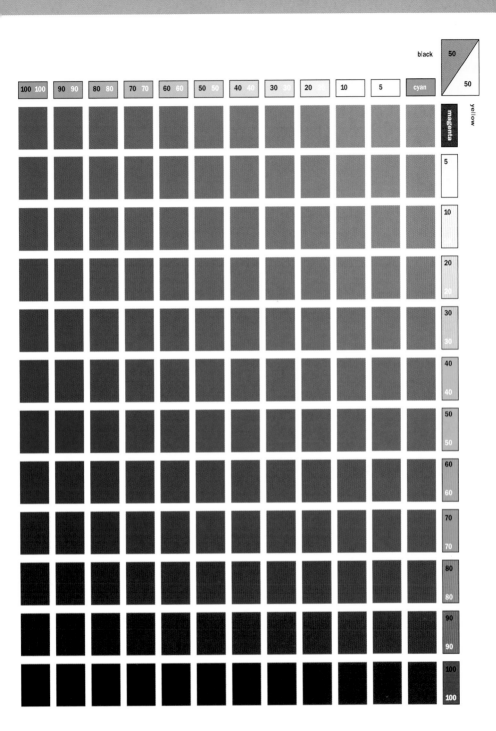

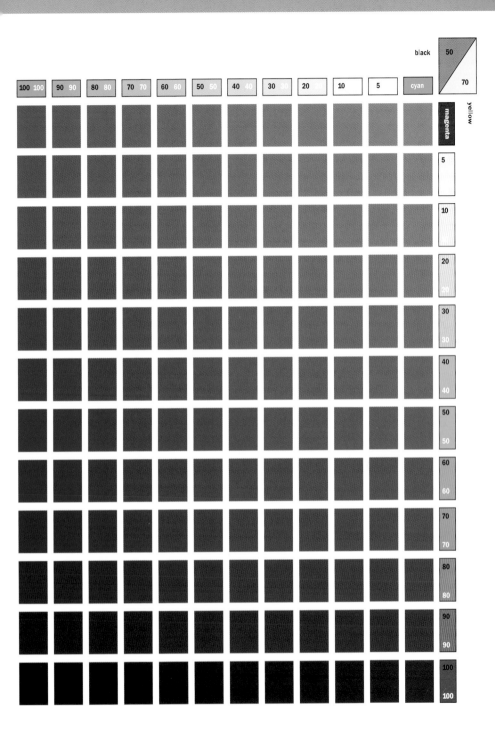

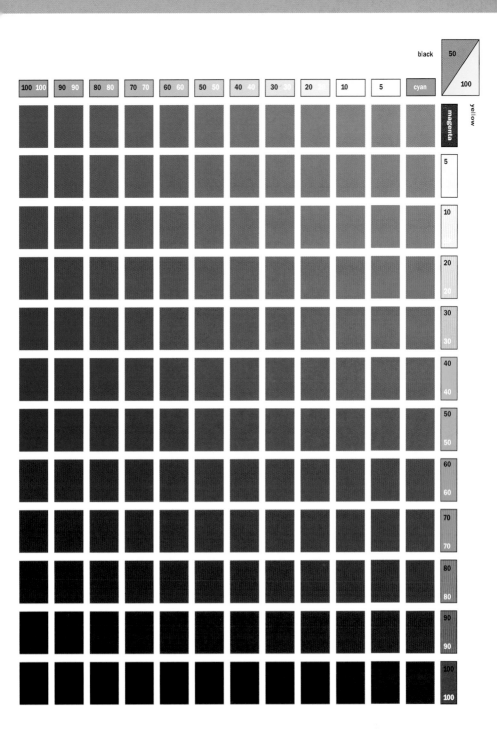

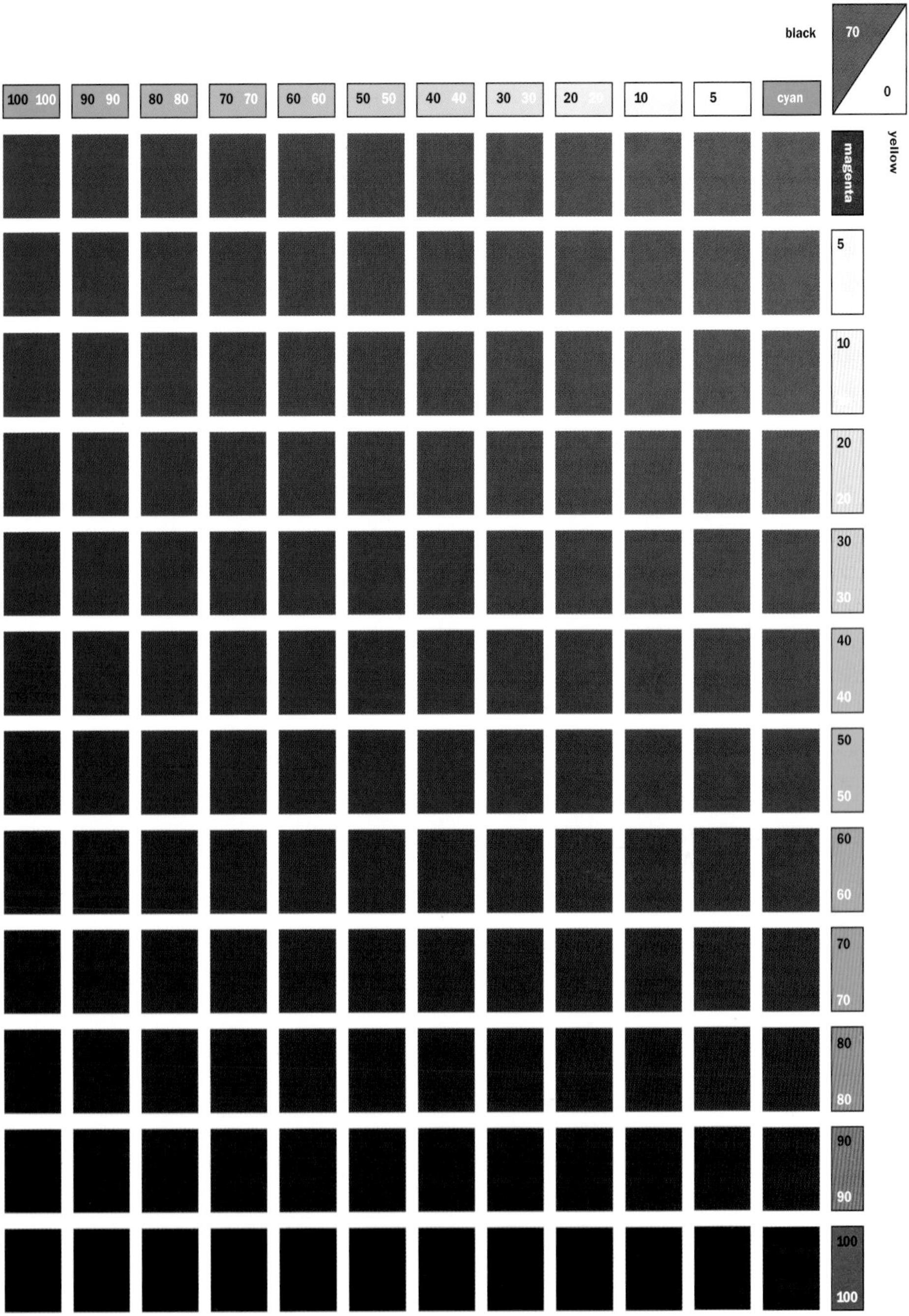

| 100 100 | 90 90 | 80 80 | 70 70 | 60 60 | 50 50 | 40 40 | 30 30 | 20 20 | 10 | 5 | cyan |
|---------|-------|-------|-------|-------|-------|-------|-------|-------|----|---|------|

magenta

5

10

20

20

30

30

40

40

50

50

60

60

70

70

80

80

90

90

100

100

| 100 100 | 90 90 | 80 80 | 70 70 | 60 60 | 50 50 | 40 40 | 30 30 | 20 20 | 10 | 5 | cyan |
|---|---|---|---|---|---|---|---|---|---|---|---|

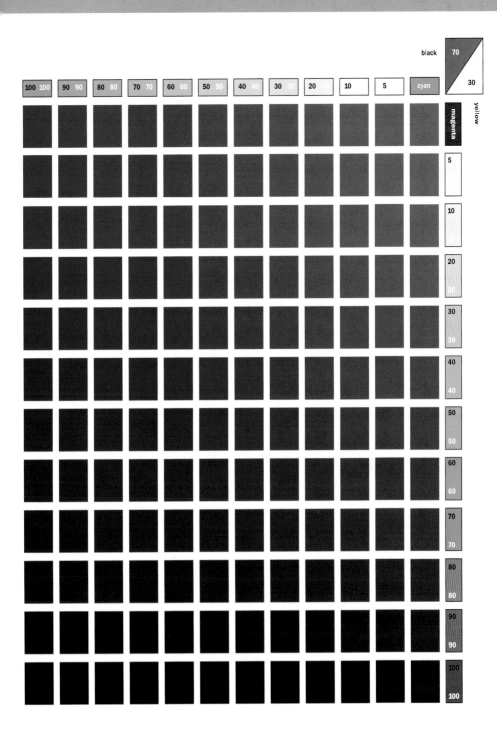

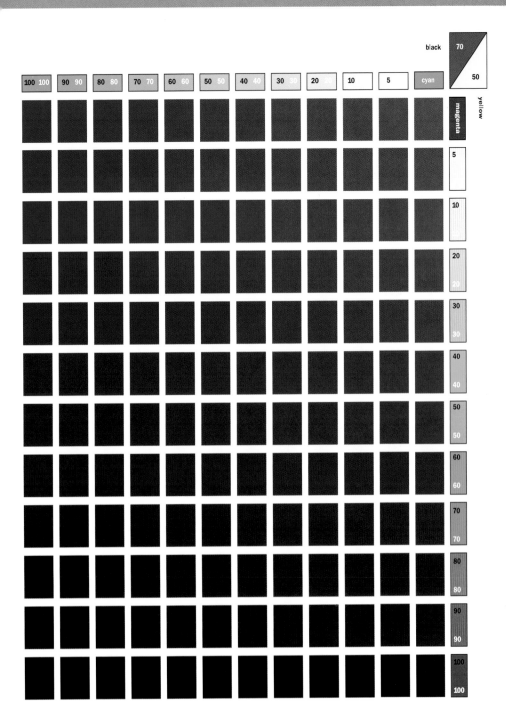

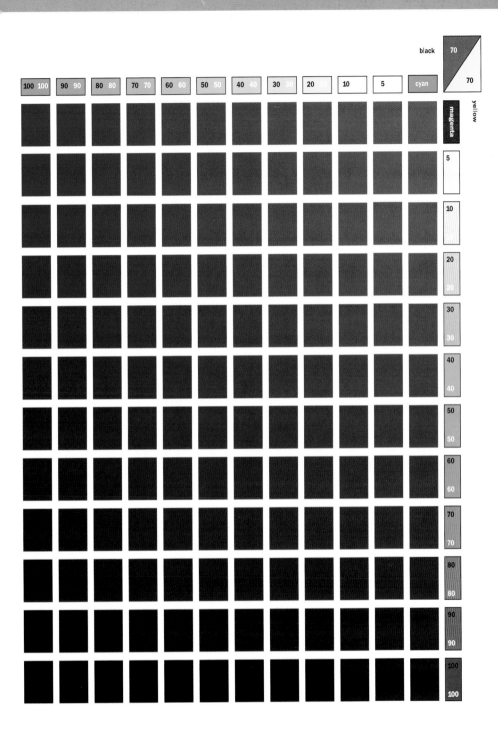

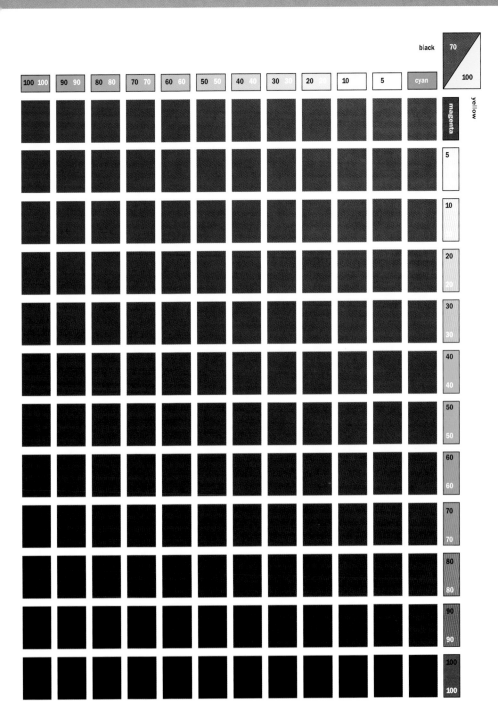

# Index

# About the Author

Poppy Evans is an award-winning writer and graphic designer. She has written more than 200 articles, which have appeared in *Print*, *HOW*, *Step Inside Design*, and other design trade magazines. She is also the author of thirteen books, including *The Designer's Survival Handbook*, *Exploring the Elements of Design*, and *Extraordinary Graphics for Unusual Surfaces*. She is assistant professor of communication arts at the Art Academy of Cincinnati and lives in Park Hills, Kentucky.

ACKNOWLEDGMENTS

Thanks to the following individuals whose expertise helped greatly in compiling information for this book:

Michaelle Keyes, Landor Associates

Ellen Weaver, Digitas LLC

Valerie Lucio, USPS

Kim McKnight, Cincinnati Graphic Coatings